Getting to Excellent

HOW TO CREATE BETTER SCHOOLS

Getting to Excellent

HOW TO CREATE BETTER SCHOOLS

Judith A. Langer

TEACHERS
COLLEGE
PRESS

Teachers College, Columbia University
New York and London

Published by Teachers College Press, 1234 Amsterdam Avenue, New York, NY 10027

Library of Congress Cataloging-in-Publication Data

Langer, Judith A.
    Getting to excellent : how to create better schools / Judith A. Langer.
      p. cm.
    Includes bibliographical references and index.
    ISBN 0-8077-4473-5 (cloth : alk. paper) —ISBN 0-8077-4472-7 (pbk. : alk. paper)
    1. School improvement programs—United States. 2. School management and organization—United States. I. Title.

  LB2822.82.L36 2004
  371.2—dc22   2004043973

ISBN 0-8077-4472-7 (paper)
ISBN 0-8077-4473-5 (cloth)

Printed on acid-free paper

Manufactured in the United States of America

11 10 09 08 07 06 05 04   8 7 6 5 4 3 2 1

To my sons Richard and Gary,
to their families,
and to our future generations.

Contents

Preface ix

1 Successful Schools Follow a Different Drummer 1

The National Focus 2
What Else? 3

2 Tests Are Used to Enrich the Curriculum, Not to Narrow It 8

Using Tests as an Opportunity 10
Setting Broad Learning Goals 12
Preparing for Tests 14
Building Curriculum 15
Spending Time and Money 16
Excellent Schools: What's the Difference? 17

3 Investing in Professionalism Pays Off 19

A Professional Community at School 21
Professionalism Within and Beyond the School 24
Making Things Happen 25
Respect for Learning 27
Professionalism in Schools That Work 28

4 The Academic Program Gets Frequent Tune-Ups 30

The Academic Program Within the Department 31
The Academic Program Within the Interdisciplinary Team 33
Organizing What Gets Taught: The Big Picture 34
Extra Help 37
Academic Programs in Effective Schools: How They Work 40

5 Instruction Aims High and Is Responsive to Students 42

Aiming High 43
Teaching Students What to Do 46
Teaching Skills 48
Improved Instruction 51

6   Parents, Community, and Schools Work Together—Really   53

   School Management   *54*
   Children's School Lives   *57*
   School Offerings Within and Beyond the School   *59*
   The School as a Community Resource   *62*
   Caring Counts, Too   *63*

7   Good Schools Are Possible Everywhere:
    One Neighborhood, Two Schools   65

   The Neighborhood   *66*
   The Schools   *66*
   The Parents and Community   *68*
   Different Responses to Tests   *69*
   Different Notions of Professionalism   *71*
   Different Academic Programs   *72*
   Different Kinds of Instruction   *73*
   The Two Schools: A Re-View   *75*

8   The Road to Change   77

   What Teachers Can Do   *81*
   What School Administrators Can Do   *83*
   What Parents Can Do   *85*
   What Next?   *86*

9   Frequently Asked Questions   89

   Home Decisions   *90*
   Connecting with School   *95*
   Why Things Get Taught That Way   *99*
   Special Needs   *103*
   In Closing   *106*

Appendix: About the Study   107

Notes   113

Index   119

About the Author   129

Preface

THIS IS MY TENTH book, following a 5-year study of effective instruction. I began the study because I wanted to help schools get through this high-stakes testing era and also to help students gain the higher literacy I think counts so much in today's society. My goal was to learn about the kinds of professional lives teachers lead, the kinds of instruction students receive, and the overall school environments and community relations that exist in more as opposed to less effective schools. The differences are remarkable—and helpful, I think—for those who wish to make their schools work better.

I've written several academic papers reporting my finding and have spoken to many groups across the country about the work and its implications for changing schools. Audiences and colleagues have urged me to write a more general book. They've told me the work is timely and of interest to everyone who has a stake in education: administrators, teachers, and other educational leaders of course, but also parents, employers, community members, legislators and taxpayers—everybody. And my son Gary has been after me for several years to write for a broader audience. As the parent of two young children, he's convinced me I have much to say that parents like him want and need to hear. I listened. I took a sabbatical to write, and here it is. I hope it will be of interest.

In addition to Gary, who gave important feedback on earlier drafts, I have many people to thank. The study took place in 88 classes in four states. For in-depth detailed research, that's a lot. We were in classrooms several weeks a year for 2 years each and in e-mail and phone contact with teachers and other school personnel weekly. I can't thank the educators enough for putting up with our intrusions. I hope this book and the other pieces I've written in some way compensate for their cooperation. I also want to thank the field researchers who worked hard and long and traveled far to gather the data. They are Paola Bonissone, Sallie Jo Bronner, Carla Confer, Gladys Cruz, Ester Helmar-Salasoo, Tanya Manning, Eija Rougle, and Anita Stevens. I couldn't have done without them. I'd also like to thank those at the Center on English Learning & Achievement: Janet Angelis, Betty Close, Jill Harbeck, Laura Morill, Mary Murphy, and the rest of the CELA staff. They're the best research institute team imaginable, a dream team. Of course I want to thank the people at the Institute of Education Sciences (IES) in the U.S. Department of Education who funded the project, especially Rita Foy, our project monitor, who oversaw its development and supported the work every step of the way. Thanks are inadequate for my most cherished colleague, Arthur Applebee.

A special tribute to Eileen and Robert Self for hosting me in Provence heaven, where, in beauty and solitude, I had the good fortune to write this book.

J.A.L.
Cotignac, France

Getting to Excellent

HOW TO CREATE BETTER SCHOOLS

Successful Schools Follow
a Different Drummer

OPEN THE DOORS and walk inside. You'll know a successful school right away. Look at the hallway walls, inside the classrooms and offices, and into the meeting areas. These are the best places to see how schools are working. They show where and how learning happens, how professional knowledge and planning work, even the extent of community involvement. They also show how students learn effectively—or don't. Excellent schools are schools that work well. They're effective. They look and feel different from others, and the teachers, administrators, and students work differently in them. This book describes what makes them different. It's for teachers, schools administrators, and policymakers, parents, community members, employers, and elected officials—everyone who's interested in education and wants to see improvement. It will show you how effective schools work and what you can do to help improve your own schools.

This is a momentous time for education in the United States, and we need to use it well. We're in the midst of a national focus on the quality of learning in the nation's schools. The current debates about curricular content, standards, and high-stakes testing are important and well intentioned. But we've heard such debates before in our history, and the concerns and problems have outlived the debates each time. If we want this time to be different, our attention needs to focus on a different set of issues. We need to look at the reality of what teachers, administrators, and communities do to make a difference in student learning.

Concern about the quality of our schools isn't new, but it has become widespread enough to rise to the top of the nation's agenda. Employers have been voicing concern that too many high school graduates can't read or write well enough to meet job demands. African American and Hispanic parents have been protesting that their children's needs are not being met— that there is an unacceptable gap between the performance of their children and that of White students. Ongoing studies, notably the "Nation's Report Card," from the National Assessment of Educational Progress, underscore the persistent color and poverty gaps in educational achievement—and also the fact that precious few students from *any* group are reaching the highest levels of performance.

Discontent with our schools has been fueled by social and political forces. Awareness of the problem would be insufficient, were it not buttressed by a public sense of civic involvement and demand for change. And the political forces gain power from a new cross-party consensus on the need for tighter standards and accountability. George W. Bush deftly focused on education in the 2000 election and beyond, demonstrating the political appeal of an aggressive education reform policy. The pressure of public demand on one side, and political opportunity on the other, has produced a critical mass for change.

THE NATIONAL FOCUS

Two movements are shaping current reform efforts. One focuses on the development of state and national standards to upgrade curriculum and teaching in the major subjects; the other uses high-stakes tests to more closely track student progress in these subjects more closely. This culminated in 2001 in the passage of an education bill called the No Child Left Behind Act, supported jointly by the conservative President Bush and the liberal Senator Edward Kennedy of Massachusetts. That legislation calls for annual tests in reading and mathematics in grades 3–8, as well as science assessments to be administered once at each level: elementary, middle, and high school. And this law has teeth; results have potential programmatic, funding, and oversight consequences for both students and schools.[1]

There is no doubt that large-scale testing has essential uses. It's the only way to establish a baseline and track progress of student performance. But is testing a panacea? Critics have their doubts. They say testing time takes days away from instructional time, forces a focus on coverage of items rather than depth of understanding, stifles teacher creativity and curricular innovations, measures outcomes without considering inputs, and encourages rote learning. Such concerns are growing; despite the widespread support for improved education, there have been some negative reactions to the increased amount of testing and its consequences.[2] In 1999, even before the bill had been introduced, parent groups in at least 12 states demonstrated outside state capitols and held local protest meetings in resistance to uses of already ratcheted-up statewide testing programs. Twenty busloads of parents from New York City traveled to Albany to protest a statewide testing mandate. In Scarsdale, an affluent suburb of New York City, 65 percent of the eighth-grade class boycotted the science exam. In Massachusetts, hundreds of students boycotted the state exam and traveled to the state capitol with 7,000 signatures. Parent protest meetings echoed from Maine to California.[3] Even after the federal bill had been passed, the commissioner of education in New Jersey, whose governor had campaigned on a pledge to rein in standardized testing, announced his intention to scale back the subjects to reading, writing, and mathematics.[4]

Some studies and polls show that by and large parents say they're happy with the kind of education their children are getting at the schools they attend. They see the problems they read about as being somewhere else. Yet on the basis of the new federal law, whether parents are happy with their local schools or not, those with students performing under certain benchmarks will have to offer particular services and undertake various remedies. How parents will react to changes in their local schools is yet to be seen.

WHAT ELSE?

The bottom line is that it takes more than testing to make good schools. For all the long-running debate about education in the United States, the roar of public concern and the rush of policymaking, something crucial gets missed: the professional efforts and classroom strategies that together build the life of a school. We need to look at them if we're going to understand where and why learning happens and how students succeed. We've all seen reforms come and go, without much impact on the fundamental problems. The problem now, as in the past, is that we haven't tackled the entire instruction and learning complex—professional growth, the mechanisms for making changes, and ways to carry them out—that goes into what students experience, think about, and learn on a daily basis. Far better for us to seize this moment in history to try a new approach in which we think of education as a set of interconnected processes, one that intimately involves the district, school, and community as well as the students and teachers and what happens in their classrooms.

I recently completed a 5-year study aimed at identifying just such an approach to literacy education—to developing students' ability to read, write, and use language in ways that let them learn successfully and communicate with others. Literacy is the backbone of what it means to be an educated person. At school, it underpins everything. The results of my study tell us a lot about how effective schools work and give us a vision for the changes needed to make less effective schools better.[5] I began the work already knowing that many schools across the country have earned good reputations for helping their students do better in reading, writing, and English. But some schools have been far more successful than others like them, even others that are similar demographically.[6] What happens in more successful schools in comparison to less successful ones that have similar students, communities, and budgets? Are there differences in the ways teachers stay on top of their profession, keep up with the times, and do what they think is best for their students? Are there differences in the curriculum and ways of teaching? Are there particular ways the more effective schools go about ensuring that they're being responsive to the public outcry for improved learning, in comparison to those that are trying hard but with less effect?

Because the nation's schools have been given a mandate to change, I wanted my study to provide some guidance to educators, parents, and policymakers about critical features that make a difference—that help some schools and states beat the odds. Along with my project team, I studied 88 middle and high school English and language arts classes in a range of communities, in four states, for 2 years each.[7] Reading and literacy as well as English and language arts teachers were involved. We followed the teachers into their classrooms as well as to their various formal and informal professional activities. We wanted to learn the factors both inside and outside the classroom that have an impact on what gets taught, how, and what that means for student learning. Because some schools were organized into interdisciplinary academies, teams, and teaching partnerships, the backdrop of the study extended beyond the confines of the English program (see Chapter 4, for examples). Further, because we studied the ways in which approaches to instructional improvement were taking place, we had the opportunity to see the ways in which not only the professional educators but also the parents and community members were invited into or kept apart from the investigations, plans, and changes taking place. This book is based on the full set of analyses, drawing on findings not reported elsewhere. While the findings can be taken as a guide for action, they need to be interpreted and used in light of the particular situations, subject matter, and problems at hand. From this vantage point, I think the results have the potential to fundamentally reshape our thinking about educational change and, by extension, to help build new solutions to our schools' long-running problems.

Did the findings bring any surprises? Oh, yes. We all have expectations about what schools should look like and do. Our expectations are often influenced by the kinds of schools we went to and teachers we had, as well as the stories about school we read when we were young and the ways we played school with our friends. Here are some common expectations:

- Our home and school lives are separate. Parents offer to help when needed (such as field trips) but otherwise keep out of the way.
- Administrators set policy and teachers teach. Teachers worry about their students and what happens in their classrooms, while administrators have primary responsibility for the overall curriculum, testing, and outreach to parents.
- When test scores are important, class is a time for practice, practice, practice; the usual studies are set aside and review and cramming begin.
- During class, we listen to the teacher and answer questions about facts we need to know, with less attention to using those facts as a way to increase our understanding of the larger issues about the subject or being taught ways to become more effective learners ourselves.
- The curriculum and teaching approaches our teachers use are pretty much the same as in the past and rarely change unless a problem occurs.
- Some students don't learn as well as others and need a different curriculum.

In our studies, we found one group of schools that closely resembled this set of expectations. Curiously, however, these were the schools that were performing only typically. But there was a second set of schools that violated most of these expectations. And they were the excellent schools, those that worked well.

In the rest of this book, I discuss the differences between programs that are simply typical and those that are more successful. The differences are outstanding—important for us to consider from the outset as we contemplate the kinds of changes we are asking schools to make. Overall, you will see that although educators—and policymakers and parents—are trying to identify and latch onto "best practices," it is less the particular curriculum or particular teaching methodologies that make the difference than the ways in which school life gets orchestrated, teachers keep up to date, class is experienced, and students learn.

While teacher creativity and school management count, they are not enough. Having a few wonderful teachers in a school is not enough. More effective schools look and feel different; they are marked by an overriding sense of knowledge, coherence, organization, and caring. Teachers and administrators learn what's needed, work toward common goals, get ongoing feedback, and grow professionally. They are marked by professional and local communities that see to it that students have connected, built-upon, and thought-provoking experiences across classes and over time.

From the moment you step inside, whatever the demographics might be, the more effective schools are welcoming, competent, collaborative, and professionally involved. A walk through the halls shows pride of learning and a sense of continuity. Peeking into the classrooms shows students sometimes working alone, sometimes in groups or in whole class; sometimes quiet, sometimes active, often talking with one another, but always mentally engaged. That is a really big difference. The students in the more effective schools are mentally engaged with school content most of the time. They are not merely sitting in class and being obedient—they are actually "minds on," engaging with real ideas more of the time. Students see school as a place to learn and actively participate.

Just as the students are mentally engaged, so, too, are the teachers. Teachers are treated as professionals who, as in any field, need to assess how things are going, keep ahead of the knowledge they need, and play an active role in making decisions and monitoring change.

The local community, including parents as well as local residents and businesses, also plays a role in the school's success. Parents and community members talk about students' needs, the public agenda, the school's response to it, and the role they can and do play. School plans of action are put into place based on the particulars of the local community as well as state and national goals.

Expectations are different, too. Every day, year in and out, there is the belief that all students can learn and that the professional staff must find ways to make that happen.

This is not to say that excellent schools don't have problems. Of course they do. They have budgetary problems, teachers disagree, some innovations don't work. Their problems are not unlike those of other schools, but they deal with them differently—proactively, collaboratively.

In each chapter to follow, I focus on an important set of features that distinguishes more effective from less effective schools, even when both are trying hard to improve student learning. You'll read about a number of schools I've chosen for variety. But they aren't isolated cases. For any one I talk about, many others like them show the same features. Your schools can be like them, too. I hope the issues I raise and the examples I give will be useful to everyone interested in seizing the moment and making this a time for major educational change, rather than grasping for fix-ups that won't be as effective in the long run.

Tests Are Used to Enrich the Curriculum, Not to Narrow It

TESTING IS THE HOT issue today—the one educators, parents, and the public seem most concerned about. But our assumptions about tests do not necessarily match up with reality. For instance, most of us remember cramming for tests when we were in school, and we think it works. We may also assume that a test, in and of itself, truly can tell how well a student is doing. We forget that there are many kinds of tests and that each type tells us different things. We also forget what common sense and research tell us— that one test can never reveal everything a student has learned. Nor does cramming shore up learning.

Consider the reading and writing exams students across the United

States take to demonstrate their literacy learning; they're not all the same. Even the high-stakes competency tests most states now require are very different from state to state. Some focus more on literature, some more on the presentation of information. Some ask students to write an essay about what they've read; others ask multiple-choice questions about content, grammar, and usage as well as content. Some want to see longer pieces of student writing; some don't. Some are interested in vocabulary knowledge and oral fluency; some are not. The particular literacy behaviors they wish to tap differ.

Further, although we all think we know what literacy is, it's a slippery term. Throughout this book I use the term to mean students' growing ability to read with understanding, write effectively, use language flexibly, and learn with and from a range of written and oral texts and media. But its meaning varies depending on the time, place, and situation a person is in. As a result, statistics we read about literacy can easily be misleading, although not necessarily intentionally so. We need to understand the results of literacy tests in terms of time, place, people, communication systems, technologies, and values. And these are always changing. From this vantage point, the tests that are given and the benchmarks for judging student performance are not necessarily better or worse today than they were in the past. Instead, they reflect societal goals, concerns, and needs that most people identify with today. Although, as in the past, they're likely to change in the future, such tests are part of the reality of today's schools and must be taken seriously by teachers, administrators, children, and parents.

Some parents as well as educators fear that an increased focus on testing means that enriched curriculum and engaging school projects will be dropped in favor of test preparation.[1] That need not be the case. There are essential differences in the ways higher-performing schools respond to the increased focus on testing in comparison to more typical schools. Whether or not curriculum and activities are curtailed depends on how the administrators and teachers in a particular school respond to the test. If they prepare students in the ways the higher-performing schools we studied did, the enriched programs can continue and their children will do better, both on the tests and in their broader coursework.

In short:

- No one test can tell how well a student is doing.
- Tests are time-sensitive—artifacts of time, place, societal goals, and technologies.
- Being responsive to tests does not involve curtailing the curriculum.

USING TESTS AS AN OPPORTUNITY

Successful individuals and businesses look forward to new opportunities, and when they meet up with a problem they try to use it to their advantage, as a lever in their already forward trajectory. Similarly, schools that work well have been using this era of high-stakes testing as an opportunity to do what good educators always want to do, improve student learning. And when they get that improvement, they up the ante, aiming to enrich and extend students' experiences, applications, interests, and learning. Teachers and administrators come together to understand the test demands, what their students know and need, and how these fit into their long-term educational goals. Then they develop a plan of action.

On the other hand, while more typical schools also work hard to improve students' scores, they go about it differently. Administrators decide what programs the students need and what professional development the teachers need. The teachers are expected to enact someone else's decisions about how to improve test performance. They aren't involved in studying past or related tests and their students' needs, nor are they involved in deciding what kinds of professional development activities might help them most. Perhaps causing this hierarchical approach to the problem or perhaps as a result, the administrators and teachers in these more typical schools see the high-stakes tests as a hurdle. They treat tests as if they're something to be gotten over for the moment, followed by a level run, rather than part of the ongoing self-scrutiny and constant retooling their higher-performing colleagues consider routine. Both more successful and more typical schools work hard but, as you can see, very differently.

Let's take Parklane Middle School[2] in a large Texas city as an example. It's an urban school in the midst of a busy shopping center, a neighborhood school that draws students from middle-class residential areas as well as low-rent housing. Forty-six percent of Parklane's students receive free lunches, and it has a cultural mix of students: 47 percent Hispanic, 38 percent White, 13 percent African American, and 2 percent Asian. It's an exemplary school—bright, friendly, and well run, with happy and engaged students and teachers. Parklane students always score higher than their counterparts in other schools with similar demographics.

Parklane teachers and administrators use their own high standards to inform their response to statewide high-stakes tests rather than using the tests to dictate what to do. Rachel Kahn,[3] the curriculum coordinator, believes in getting everyone together for self-study—to examine what they're doing, how well it's working and for whom, and what else is needed for student growth. She's done it for years. She and the teachers have always worked to improve instruction and test performance. They always want to offer the best program possible and for their students to do as well as possible. When the standards and high-stakes testing program were put into place in their state, they merely continued their routine—adding the new issues to their existing list of concerns. In preparation for the exam, Rachel and the teachers studied the standards and the sample test items the state released to became familiar with their demands. They met within and across grades in the English language arts department and also within grades across subject areas. They reworked their curriculum goals and developed activities they felt were right to support high literacy development for their students. They were after a range of activities they could use throughout the school year. They tried out their new activities, discussed how their students responded to them, and honed them. They called a meeting with parents to tell them about the tests and help them become familiar with what their children would need to learn to do well. They had never seen the actual tests that would be administered, but close to the testing date, they gave students some practice with the test format and discussed test strategies with them. When the test scores arrived months later, teachers across the grades met and together analyzed how their students had done. This helped them rethink their activities through the filter of student performance. "Why do you think this was a problem for them? How does it connect with what we've been doing? Let's look at the curriculum and the activities we've developed. Is this a problem in the students' other literacy practices? What else can we do?" Each year, as test scores come in, they begin the process anew. Needs are addressed. And where the students are doing well, the team looks for ways to enrich their school experiences even further.

The Miami/Dade County Public Schools,[4] with a large and varied student body, took similar steps across some of its schools. The school district already had in place a strong English language arts supervisory team that met and worked regularly with teachers to understand how students were doing to improve instruction. Standard operating procedure included keeping up with the field, examining student progress, self-study of instructional effectiveness, and setting new goals. When the Florida state writing and later the state reading tests were developed, Norma Bossard, the districtwide director of English language arts, her supervisory staff who were assigned to work with the schools, and teachers from those schools met. They studied the tests and the demands they made on students and used their analyses to rethink the curriculum. What more should they teach? What else? What should they do differently and when? Together they developed instructional plans and sample lessons, grade by grade, that would create year-long related experiences. The supervisors visited schools, discussed the exams and their activities with teachers, and gave demonstration lessons. Through a grant, master teachers were hired to become consultants and work with their colleagues. Departments developed their own activities and shared them. All of these activities added coherence and effectiveness to an already strong instructional program.

At Parklane, the Miami/Dade effective schools we studied, and other effective schools, the tests are used for professional growth as well as instructional change. The schools have a productive conception of how to respond to external pressure for change. Because they're always in a cycle of self-inspection, analysis, professional growth, and experimentation, they use the public concerns and state tests as an excuse to rev up the cycle, to examine their efforts more closely. Even when they don't necessarily agree with the particular high-stakes test their students must take or with the kind of accountability (e.g., high school graduation) for which it is used, they seize the professional moment. They use the tests to their advantage, as a way to understand what else they need to know in order to refuel their curriculum, improve instruction, and produce the best in high literacy development for their students.

In short:

- When interpreting tests, focus on important knowledge and skills required to do the activities effectively rather than on the particular items being tested.
- Support teachers in learning ways to interpret results in terms of their own students, their classroom performance, and the curriculum.
- Incorporate what is learned from test results about students' knowledge and skills needs into the school's ongoing self-evaluation and improvement plan.
- Create working teams of professionals at your school to understand test demands; study student needs; and plan for, make and monitor change.

SETTING BROAD LEARNING GOALS

Effective schools also use tests as a way to identify broad learning goals they need to aim for. For starters, the teachers don't just administer their students' tests—they take them if they're available or old state-released ones if they're not. They do this as an act of professional inquiry; it puts them in the user's seat and lets them know firsthand the kinds of content, skills, and knowledge their students will need to think about and use. In their analyses, they avoid the trap of simply listing the specific topics or texts that are covered, the particular activities that are presented (e.g., reading and comparing two passages; discussing theme or analyzing characters), and the particular kinds of writing asked for (e.g., narration, description, explanation, persuasion) and then setting about to teach them. They go an important step further, identifying the deeper kind of knowledge that lets students succeed at the task. Then, for their teaching targets, they focus on what it takes to do well not only on the particular test but also in the literacy activities students need to use at school and home. To make its way into the curriculum, a skill or knowledge can't be confined to a particular test; it must be pervasive or generalizable enough to be useful in other situations. Having decided what knowledge and skills are important, teachers and administrators inspect and reconfigure their curriculum. Everything they do is with an eye toward helping their students learn the underlying knowledge and skills that will "pay off" not only in good test performance but also in situations beyond the test.

Overall, professionals in schools that work well know that tests aren't intended to be used to dictate curriculum but rather to sample performance from a much larger range of knowledge students are learning. If that larger array of knowledge is well taught and well learned, students should do well on any tests they must take. This viewpoint liberates teachers and administrators to decide what they need to do to ensure effective teaching and learning, including the kinds of professional growth and instructional development they need to make it work.

But more typical schools are more reactive and narrower in their scope of action. They see the tests as a blueprint to follow, and they prepare for tests by practicing old test packets (when available) or testlike facsimiles, and they organize their instruction around the content, text types, and writing assignments the tests call for. They not only alter their curriculum but also narrow it to correspond to the particular items presented in the high-stakes test. George Hillocks, education professor at the University of Chicago, recently completed a study of writing tests that underscores this problem. He found that when teachers know less about ways to teach writing to their students, they rely on the tests as their basis for teaching.[5]

In short:

- Don't let tests narrow your educational goals; they are only a sampling of everything students need to learn.
- Concentrate on the big picture—on the skills and knowledge needed to do well at school and in life as well as on the test.
- A challenging and enriched curriculum beats one that has been altered to focus primarily on getting ready for the test.

PREPARING FOR TESTS

Schools that work well know that good performance in class doesn't always translate into ability to do well on the test; knowledge of content and skills is sometimes not enough to get through. Therefore, they help students become familiar with the test format a few weeks before the test (like Parklane) or lightly intersperse the test format into a more general set of activities across the year. But there is little other focus on the tests themselves. Instead, the day-to-day activities at the heart of the curriculum get the attention; the better the activities are, the more likely the payoff. Test prep isn't at all the traditional cram-the-content and drill-the-format so many of us remember. Instead, teachers integrate what it takes to do well into the curriculum across the year (and across the grades). While they also teach the test format and test-taking skills separately and highlight them before the test, the real preparation for the test of literacy is embedded over the year into the larger set of ongoing and more generally useful classroom activities.

But many schools don't work this way. More typical schools work very hard at another kind of test prep, where test formats and test answers become ends unto themselves and the goal is merely to help students do better on the high-stakes tests. Because the spotlight is on the scores, they think that more and more practice on testlike content and formats will get their students through. Much of the usual curriculum is set aside for pseudo test work. It's well meant, but it gets more limited results both on the tests and in helping students gain higher literacy. When the tests change, they're in trouble. I saw that happen in some schools that drilled students in persuasive writing for several years because the writing exam asked for a persuasive essay. And when the state test changed to ask for another kind of writing, they were back where they had started. The schools that revved up their curriculum as part of the district plan focused instead on helping their students understand the various purposes for writing, of which writing to persuade was only one kind. This got them through the persuasive essay when called for and left them in good shape when the test changed. It also helped them become better writers in the range of genres they'll need for life. These students had learned more.

In short:

- Enrich, don't cram.
- Don't shape class work for a particular test or you'll be in trouble when the items or format change.
- Offer a challenging curriculum with activities that give students practice in learning and using knowledge that is at the heart of the particular subject rather than the particular test.

BUILDING CURRICULUM

Many successful schools and districts use the tests and standards to rework their curriculum. Like her counterparts in other effective districts, Parklane's districtwide language arts supervisor has been working collaboratively with teachers across her district to become familiar with state standards and the state tests. Together, they've written a draft curriculum that the teachers in each school can use as they work together to refine their own departmental efforts. She tries to get feedback from all teachers, and the curriculum is a work in progress. Parklane teachers were on the districtwide committee, and the materials they helped develop have become another set of professional tools for them to use with their colleagues, discuss at meetings, and integrate into their curriculum in ways that are adapted to their school and students.

There are many different ways in which such activities can be organized and supported. Foshay Learning Center,[6] a middle school in Los Angeles, has undertaken a curriculum- and instruction-building project in which the district identifies teachers to be "intern instructors" who work with a state curriculum supervisor in collaboration with a neighboring university. They attend workshops to learn strategies for integrating state standards into the ongoing curriculum. Then they work collaboratively with their school colleagues, using the approaches they learned as a way to integrate the standards and test goals into the curriculum and at the same time refuel it. As at Miami/Dade and Parklane, the goal is to use the test as an opportunity to improve both the curriculum and instructional activities.

Even students are helped to look at the big picture. Kate McFadden-Midby, at Foshay, feels it's important for teachers to understand how students react to the tests they must take. Therefore, she lets her students take an old test, explains the way it's constructed, what the different test sections are trying to focus on, and how last year's class had done overall. She asks students for their feedback on what they find easy and difficult and what kind of help they feel they can use. She makes connections between the test and other reading and writing activities they do. Then she integrates many of the student concerns into her already rich activities.

Some teachers help their students become familiar with the scoring criteria that are used by the state to judge student writing. They discuss what it takes to get the highest score and why these features are considered important components of good writing. Then students learn to judge pieces they've read as well as those they write. They become critics, internalizing components of better writing. All this feeds into students' growing ability to evaluate and fine-tune their own writing, on tests and for other purposes.

But too many schools believe they need to zoom in on test particulars, to narrow the curriculum and drill for the tests. They fear that not doing so will be time away from test preparation. A survey of the ways teachers have responded to standards and high-stakes testing in Colorado[7] found that curriculum and instruction have changed substantially. The Colorado teachers—like those in the typical schools I studied—reported that while they have increased the time spent on test preparation activities, they have also eliminated field trips and extended projects.

In short:

- Use student performance on tests and in class as well as tests and standards to rework the curriculum.
- Treat the curriculum as an ongoing work-in-progress.
- After testing, get students' views of what was easy for them, what they could do with effort, and what they had difficulty with.
- Involve teachers and administrators in curriculum-building and instructional development projects.

SPENDING TIME AND MONEY

It may come as no surprise that with similar demographics, by and large excellent schools operate with budgets similar to those in schools that are more typical.[8] They just spend their money in very different ways. They spend more on professional growth and on collaborative development of instructional projects, as you will see in Chapters 3 and 4. Teachers are sent to professional meetings and encouraged to visit schools they think will give them new ideas. Speakers are brought in to discuss particular topics of concern. Teachers are directly involved in selecting instructional materials and are given time to plan, try out, and discuss instructional activities of all sorts. Administration's goal is to offer teachers the experiences they need in order to think through and carry out what is needed to do their jobs well, with improved test scores as one goal. And they are willing to pay for it.

For example, I'm often invited to speak to school district committees and larger gatherings about the results of my studies. At professional conferences I speak more generally, but at district meetings I can focus on the particular situation. Usually I'm given a topic to discuss based on their problems (e.g., what can poor inner city schools do to raise scores) and members of the audience come with prepared questions. Often the discussion takes precedence over my presentation and is followed by small-group discussions giving people a chance to talk about the ideas in relation to their students and schools. Such investments in ongoing professional development have a continuing payoff in the quality of teaching and learning.

More typical schools spend money on a variety of practice tests, fix-up materials, and activities that are written or delivered by others, without really changing the teachers' deep professional knowledge about instruction, students' needs, testing—or how they all interact. These schools don't make a substantive change in the curriculum or in the instructional approaches the students experience on a daily basis. The administrators and teachers try to be responsive to the tests, want students to do better, and most often take action, but they lack the systemic, organized, highly informed, communicative, and participatory features that pervade the more successful schools.

In short:

- Invest in keeping teachers and administrators up to date and involved in current research and ideas in their profession.
- Invest in collaborative inquiry—into what's needed to improve curriculum and instruction.
- Invest in improving curriculum and instruction rather than shorter-term "test prep."

EXCELLENT SCHOOLS: WHAT'S THE DIFFERENCE?

Schools that work better see the standards and testing movement as an opportunity. They see it as a manifestation of the public's desire for improved performance, and they feel they can get it. It's what they do all the time, and they take the standards and testing movement as a nudge to look again. They seem always to feel that their students can learn more and think more deeply, that they can read and write with greater fluency and sophistication—and they're open to the changes that will help them make it happen.

On the other hand, more typical schools view the standards and testing movement with trepidation. They know they must increase student performance but are less sure they'll be able to do it. That's a big difference, as we'll see in the next chapter.

First, rate your school, using the chart on the next page.

How Effective Is Your School?—Testing

		RATE YOUR SCHOOL		
MORE EFFECTIVE SCHOOLS:	**LESS EFFECTIVE SCHOOLS:**	Doing Well	Needs Improvement	Needs to Get Started
Place the spotlight on course knowledge, goals, and effectiveness.	Place the spotlight on scores.			
Use tests as an opportunity to self-inspect and to refine practice.	Use tests as a dictate to conform to what is tested.			
Engage in an ongoing cycle of analysis, professional growth, and experimentation.	Examine and rethink practices only when scores are low.			
Believe it is possible to help all students do better.	Believe some students won't or can't improve.			
Respond to tests by identifying ways to enrich what is taught.	Respond to tests by narrowing what gets taught to favor what gets tested.			
Relate the knowledge and skills tested to their uses in course-work and life.	Use tests as a blueprint to follow.			
Embed test prep into ongoing activities.	Increase time allocated to separate test prep.			
After the test, have teachers, administrators, and students tell their views of test demands in light of their coursework.	After the test, appoint supervisory staff to do test alignment, without input from teachers.			
Interpret test results in light of the students, the curriculum, and class performance.	Treat test results as solitary indicators of need.			
Form professional work groups to review test results, rethink instruction and extend goals.	Distribute test results to teachers without group review, discussion, and planning.			
Invest primarily in school-wide professional improvement to raise test scores.	Invest primarily in outside add-ons to raise test scores.			

☆ C H A P T E R 3 ☆

Investing in Professionalism
Pays Off

FROM THE OVERALL PICTURE I've sketched in the previous two chapters, it should come as no surprise that in schools that work well, teachers' professional experiences are rich and varied. In the middle of the 20th century, the psychologist Jean Piaget made us aware that young children think their teachers live at school and never go home. To their young charges, their sole existence is as teachers, and the children imagine that this role and none other continues even after the halls empty and the last child has arrived home. On the one hand, this is of course true. A professional identity never goes away. It permeates a life. But on the other, although we as adults really do know how different teachers' professional lives can be, we have stereotypes of what it means for them to be professional. We think of them in their classroom teacher role and not in the other roles they play as teachers. We ordinarily don't think about their fuller professional lives or about how the quality of those lives affects what happens in the classroom.

Like engineers, lawyers, financial consultants, and physicians, teachers' professional experiences differ based on their working environments, the people they spend time with, and the chances they have to connect with their professional organizations. In some workplaces, management considers professional collaboration and involvement critical to getting the job done well. They put teams together to understand a whole project, develop a unified plan of action, stay informed about what the others are doing, and monitor how the whole project is developing. No one is left out of the loop. The point is to make sure the parts are connected and relevant to each other, and to develop something that has internal as well as external integrity. But we all know other workplaces where employees are expected to use their expertise to do one specific part of the job, like developing a program to track inventory, without knowing about the whole environment in which it will be used or the entire project of which it is a part. Findings from my studies show that just as in other fields, the patterns in the teachers' professional lives in schools that work well are distinctly richer and more connected than those in more typical schools; the environment invites active professionalism—and it pays off in student learning.

Administrators also know that change for its own sake isn't sensible, but to do a job well, they and their teachers need always to be on the lookout for evidence that change may be needed and what it might be. For them, success on the job involves not only collaboration but also awareness of new ideas in the field and an understanding of what these imply for their own situations. Many studies have shown that teachers' knowledge about the content, their students, and ways to teach them is of central importance in how well students learn.[1] In schools that work well, administrators believe teacher knowledge makes a difference, and they create an environment that fosters professional involvement and growth within a connected and communicating professional community. In more typical schools, however, although workshops may be offered and coursework supported, what is being learned as well as if and how that knowledge can be best used becomes a deliberative and shared enterprise only when problems arise.

Teachers in more effective schools are expected to live highly collaborative and professionally involved lives. They're constantly given opportunities to keep up and grow because it's the standard, the way things get done. They consider it an integral part of what good teachers do. They're brought into work groups and given the time to keep up with their students' needs, stay current in their fields, keep an ear to the public, and stay in touch with each other. They live active and engaged professional lives both in school and out.

In short:

- Keep teachers involved in the professional life of the school, beyond their classrooms.
- Provide teachers with opportunities to discuss their professional knowledge and use it toward school improvement.
- Create a school environment that fosters professional collaboration, involvement, and growth among teachers and administrators—together.

A PROFESSIONAL COMMUNITY AT SCHOOL

Schools that work well have an enriched and highly professional working environment. You feel it the moment you visit one of these schools. You see people working with one another and sense their unity of purpose. While they're immersed in making the moment-to-moment program as rich and successful as possible, they're also reflecting on what's happening— taking notes, so to speak, about ways to make it even better next time. At the same time, they're looking beyond the good programs and instruction under way, inquiring about potentially bigger changes—trying out what else they might do to improve and enrich students' school experiences and learning. They pool their efforts, discuss what they're doing, share their own and their students' work, get ideas and give feedback about ongoing work, while also planning for the future.

Administrators and teachers actively encourage their colleagues to become and stay involved in a variety of professional communities; participating in them is part of the job expectation. They know that learning about and trying out ideas for instructional improvement are best discussed with others, gaining the benefit of reflection and analysis among colleagues.

They also believe that student learning improves best in a collegial working environment. When teachers work and learn together, they have a shared understanding of what their students need and how best to help them learn. Over time, they develop a consistent philosophy of education with its related ways of developing and interpreting instructional goals and approaches. They also develop a consistent set of experiences they and their students can build on across classes and grades. Professional networks at school (e.g., instructional teams, curriculum development groups, self-study committees, university liaisons) give them ideas and nourish them in their daily efforts (which they share with each other) as well as in their collective grand plans.

This type of involvement takes time, and administrators know it. They schedule groups of teachers for common "prep" times and close schools early for teacher development time. (At Parklane,[2] for example, teachers and administration agreed to add 20 minutes to each school day to get the extra professional meeting time.) They hire substitutes when needed. They help get things started and keep them going; they are proactive in comparison to more typical schools—where there is less involvement of all sorts, and even when groups are called together to share ideas and solve problems, participants hold back, unaccustomed to speaking up. It becomes a self-fulling prophecy that groups don't work in their schools, and the process fades away.

As I intimated in Chapter 2, Parklane administrators (and particularly the curriculum coordinator, Rachel Kahn), work hard at ensuring this kind of ongoing professional collaboration. They're always examining how things are going, with an eye to improvement. Parklane teachers are scheduled to meet once a month for team meetings, once a month for department meetings, once a month for faculty meetings, and once a week for professional development. But they meet even more often; before, during, and after school, formally as well as informally. They're continually discussing new approaches, sharing ideas, and upping the ante to help their students do better. They meet and talk about literacy within and across grade levels and across subject areas. They explore effective ways to help students and coordinate what they're doing as a way to ensure students have a coherent and related program.

Parklane teachers want to keep learning and improving, and to do things for themselves. Therefore they do research, go to meetings, and call in consultants. But they then try things out and develop what works best for their students; they find and offer new programs to the students. They keep up with new ideas in the field as well as changes in their state test. They keep talking about how their students are doing and what to do to improve. They get parents into school and find ways for them to stay involved. They applaud student and colleague successes. Teachers and administrators together have many opportunities to share what they know. If someone has been to a workshop, or served on a committee, or read an article they found useful, they're asked to report on it to the others. When something works well, they describe and discuss it. When something doesn't, they discuss that, too. When money is scarce, they apply for grants. They make things work. Teachers are never left alone to founder; someone is always there. They work together.

Similarly, Cathy Starr, a veteran seventh-grade teacher at Hudson,[3] a middle grade suburban school in upstate New York, says her district "provides the time, opportunities, and kind of environment that encourages teachers to grow together. They share their thoughts and ideas, learn from each other, expose themselves to new approaches and processes, contribute their experiences, and reflect on their own practice. The interaction with colleagues in this building is a total part of who I am." When she taught in another district 30 years ago, she says, "You came in, you did your job, and you went home. You may have said hello or [had] lunch with some people, but didn't really do an awful lot of professional sharing." Today, by contrast, "there's a lot of professional conversation that goes on here every day. Some of it is planned, some informal."

Hudson has a palpable undercurrent of professional enthusiasm. The teachers meet often in school and out, baring problems, sharing ideas, attending professional meetings both as audience and as speakers, examining student learning and existing practice, and discussing, developing, and getting feedback on changes in curriculum and instruction. Because they work together as a community, they work through the particular problems of their students in their school and also coordinate the kinds of comprehensive changes that are felt schoolwide.

These kinds of professional communities have a profound impact on how instructional programs are redesigned and how they get implemented. For example, the English supervisor in Green Path,[4] a suburban school district in Texas, invited me to speak about my studies to a districtwide committee of teachers who were investigating ways they could improve high-stakes test scores while still maintaining the best changes they had made in thought-provoking English instruction over the past 10 or so years. I came prepared with lots of information but quickly learned that they had already read my papers on the CELA (Center on English Learning & Achievement) website (http://cela.albany.edu) and wanted to use my time with them for specific purposes that they had in mind. They were an ongoing professional team that was out to gather particular information they felt they needed. They knew the bigger picture and wanted my help, not my lecture. The next 2 hours involved joint discussion around their problems and ways in which my research could provide options for them to consider. In more typical schools, speakers are invited to offer talks or workshops on issues decided upon by administrators, but teachers are left to use the information as they will, without collaborative discussion about what it means or how it might work in their situation.

In short:

- Form working groups and schedule meeting times for teachers and administrators to investigate, plan, and problem-solve.
- Reserve time at meetings for faculty and staff to share new ideas and particular successes as well as problems.

- Get everyone involved in the self-inspect/learn/try out/reflect cycle.
- Discuss research findings and teaching approaches and relate them to your students.
- Work toward developing a schoolwide philosophy of teaching and learning.

PROFESSIONALISM WITHIN AND BEYOND THE SCHOOL

As you can see, teachers in schools that work well are involved; they have an ongoing sense of professional identity and a keen sense of what's possible. Administrators know that teachers need to keep up with their fields, so that they can rethink the content and ways to teach it. They know that teacher time away from the classroom will pay off with improved programs and instruction at school. They provide the time for their teachers to become professionally active at district and state levels, to participate in curriculum review and development committees, to stay connected to the education departments of local colleges and universities, and to be actively involved in their local and national professional organizations.

Teachers in these schools participate in professional meetings and conferences, they apply for research grants, and they try out new approaches. Some write professional articles, teach workshops and courses, and get their National Board Certification,[5] a special national program that recognizes outstanding teachers who successfully complete a rigorous professional examination. Because they keep up with research on pedagogy and engage in professional debate, they become valuable partners, sought after at school, district, state, and even national levels for planning, evaluating, and implementing change. They're on committees to interpret and revise standards, examine various tests and recommend change, revise curricula, write guidelines, interact with other educators about what works for their students, help research and make decisions about change, and help decide what else needs to be done. They're a critical part of the network for programmatic reform. Because the teachers are treated as knowledgeable professionals, their schools and districts provide money to continue their professional growth as well as to help them become better informed about new approaches to specific problems at hand. They become active participants in the development and well-being of the instructional program. Their goal is to learn for action.

In more typical schools, on the other hand, professional activity away from the school is considered time off work and teachers retreat from their professions. One teacher in a middle school we studied said, "I've got to say that I don't keep nearly as abreast of what's going on in the field as I should. I've let all my professional organizations and journals lapse over the last few years [since she's been in that particular school]. I don't keep up with the research." Her school does not have the kind of professional community I have been describing. "Our department chair has a way of pushing the paper-work so that we get fair warning . . . he has a way of judging what is going to be important to the administration." But there is no professional exchange beyond the bureaucratic necessities—no gaining or sharing of ideas.

Evangeline Turner[6] is a good example of the benefits of supporting teachers' professionalism. She's a highly effective teacher in an urban Cali-fornia middle school serving a very low income community (more than 70 percent of the students are eligible for free lunches[7]) and is involved in many professional activities that keep her learning and her students growing. She's active in a variety of organizations and educational groups at the national, state, local, and school levels. She's also working on her National Board Certification. She sits on the governing boards of the National Coun-cil of Teachers of English and its California branch, and she is active in the California Writing Project and the California Literature Project. Each has played an important role in her professional growth, and she carefully chooses where to spend her time based on her own professional goals and her students' needs. She's also involved in a collaborative effort with her district and a local university to work with schools that are "failing their students," offering professional guidance and development. At school she's English department chair and special helper to the principal, who often asks her to offer workshops, particularly in ways to teach reading, writ-ing, and deeper reasoning. She's also a mentor to new teachers. All this, and she's also a highly successful classroom teacher with students who are learning well and loving it; in her classroom, you see in practice all she's learned and tries to bring to others.

In short:

- Encourage teachers and administrators to become actively involved in district, state, and national efforts to improve instruction.
- Encourage involvement in professional organizations.
- Support collaborations with local colleges and universities.
- Create a mechanism for open sharing and discussion of new ideas.

MAKING THINGS HAPPEN

Beyond the active professionalism I've described, teachers in schools that work well have a sense of agency; they use their knowledge to change things and are given license to do so. They're part of goal-directed decision-making teams. Their suggestions are taken seriously and, in collaborative environments, implemented. When a problem arises, they find remedies that are acted upon. And they pass on their positive energy and sense of purposeful action to their students.

Suzanna Matton, a Springfield High School[8] teacher in an urban California school with 2,500 students, describes the administrative style in her school this way: "It's a reform movement that does directly involve the teachers in the decision-making process. Every teacher in the school is supposed to be on a governance committee. These committees will meet and consider policy decisions. The decisions that come up before these committees are generated not by the administration but by the teachers. Teachers are involved in the development of a solution to whatever the situation might be."

At Springfield, teachers shape the curriculum, instruction, and in-school assessment. For example, teachers in the English department or in an academy (in this school, programs involve faculty from a number of disciplines in a jointly taught specialization) plan the content and organization of the program. They co-plan units, create interdisciplinary units with their colleagues in other subjects, develop curricula, and confer with one another in ways that can change how programs are organized, how they are carried through, how students progress is reviewed and special cases handled, and how test preparation proceeds.

This differs dramatically from more typical schools, where teachers rarely have a sense of agency. They don't feel permitted to act as change-makers, and even when invited to do so, they are rarely given the support needed to follow it through. Often teachers don't even know how their curriculum was developed or by whom. One teacher said, "There is a curriculum council. I believe there are some members of the rank and file, one of the union stewards, some administrators. That's pretty much where the curriculum is generated. We get our standards and also our curriculum is posted in each department office." She went on to say that she had no idea how the curriculum council works nor who the individual members are. She is not alone. In typical schools, most teachers are out of the loop.

In short:

- Give teachers opportunities and support to originate ideas, try things out, and follow them through.
- Keep teachers and administrators actively involved in joint review, development, and decision making about curriculum and instruction.

RESPECT FOR LEARNING

Successful teachers and administrators consider learning to be an integral part of their profession. They not only like to teach; they also like to learn. Educators in more effective schools foster a deep respect for lifelong learning. It's considered the standard; it's how they conduct themselves at school and live their lives. They talk about meetings they've been to, books they've read, places they've been, and courses they're taking. Sallie Snyder, who was a language arts supervisor in Miami/Dade County Public Schools[9] during the time of our study, says, "the almost daily sharing of key articles, new ideas, and successful, innovative classroom practice provides the constant wellspring that isolated meetings and conferences by their very nature cannot." In Miami/Dade, the supervisors' professional sharing extends to the ways they interact with the teachers and the teachers with each other. It's common for a teacher who has read an article or heard a speaker of interest to send memos about it to administrators as well as teachers and to bring it up at a future meeting for professional update and discussion.

Teachers in these more effective schools also talk about how they're learning and what they need to do to develop new and skills and knowledge. One common topic, for example, is how they're learning to use the Internet and interactive instructional technology, and what they need to do to get better. And they have these discussions not only with their colleagues but also with their students. Teachers become real-life learners to their students; they talk together about the processes they are going through as learners as well as what they're learning about. In this way, teachers act as role models; they show by their interest and enthusiasm that learning is an enjoyable and self-selected part of ongoing life.

Alicia Alliston,[10] a middle school teacher and literacy coach in California, is typical in her enthusiasm for learning. When she was asked what influences her teaching, she said, "The fact that I'm a learner and I enjoy being a learner . . . I think that has a huge effect on how I approach the profession of teaching. . . . I think there are many people in all kinds of professions that don't necessarily enjoy change. . . . Being a lifelong learner exhilarates me . . . the openness to change and the enjoyment I get. . . . When I think about teachers who have basically stopped learning . . . and if the world keeps changing . . . and you aren't . . . what life changes are you cutting off for you and your kids?"

In typical schools, on the other hand, teachers' learning, be it school related or personal, is invisible. Although it may occur, no one knows.

In short:

- Treat the faculty as a community of learners.
- Provide opportunities for faculty to share what they've been learning and let the students in on it, too.
- Help new ideas become part of the whole-school discourse.

PROFESSIONALISM IN SCHOOLS THAT WORK

Looking back at this chapter, we can see that schools that work have pervasive, organized, highly informed, and participatory professional environments. Professional communities like this don't exist in more typical schools. Like their counterparts in so many working environments, the teamwork is missing, and so is the common vision that arises out of working together. Resources to support collaboration and professional growth are often lacking, as is the belief that it will be money well spent. Specialists are often brought in to tell teachers what to do rather than helping them explore and examine what's best for their school and their students. Even when professional groups are formed, they tend to be hierarchical or unfocused, without a history of sharing to make the participants buy in. Often lone, excellent teachers create memorable experiences for students, but that doesn't raise scores or create truly higher-performing students—who need an array of extended, connected, and rich instructional experiences throughout their time in school.

Now, rate your school, using the chart on the next page.

How Effective Is Your School?—Professionalism

		RATE YOUR SCHOOL		
MORE EFFECTIVE SCHOOLS:	*LESS EFFECTIVE SCHOOLS:*	Doing Well	Needs Improvement	Needs to Get Started
Help teachers and administrators stay involved in learning their options and deciding what works best for their students.	Look outside for answers, rather than shoring up the professionals at school.			
Are marked by professional sharing and discussion of new experiences and knowledge.	Are cordial places where staff members interact when they have to, but primarily keep their professional experiences and new knowledge to themselves.			
Involve teachers and administrators in a shared self-study/explore/try/reflect cycle and regard it as their way to create improvement.	Rarely engage in a self-study/reflect cycle, and when they do, it is often regarded as pointless.			
Leave adequate meeting time to discuss new ideas and "what works for me," as well as problems and possible solutions.	Use meeting times primarily to focus on procedures, with little engagement of professional ideas.			
Encourage teachers and administrators to keep up with their fields, recommend articles, and discuss new ideas.	Focus on the school, not the field.			
Encourage involvement in professional organizations and local university projects.	Largely ignore professional commitments outside school.			
Value committee work at the local, state or national levels as learning experiences that will benefit the school.	Consider committee work outside school as an intrusion.			

The Academic Program Gets Frequent Tune-Ups

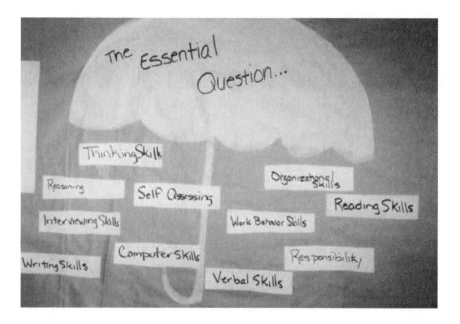

EVEN THOUGH SCHOOL organization and policies change, we often expect the academic program to stay pretty much the same (as it was when we went to school) and for changes to be made only when problems arise. From this point of view, instituting change means something's wrong, not that things are going well. On the other hand, we don't expect our good health regimes to be the same as they were 20 years ago or like those of our parents. Nor do we expect our new computer to be like our last. In this case, change is considered desirable, an expected by-product of ongoing research, new knowledge, and societal shifts. And from what I've described in the previous chapters, it should come as no surprise that schools that work well are constantly reshaping themselves to meet the needs of changing student bodies, technologies, societal demands, research findings, and the academic disciplines themselves.

We've all seen educational innovations come and go, but effective change, the kind that improves student learning over the long haul, is another matter. Larry Cuban,[1] professor of education at Stanford, likens educational change to the ocean, where waves rush over the surface and leave the underlying waters untouched. In a later book, Cuban and his colleague David Tyack argue that educational innovations don't have a good success record. Too often innovative programs are adapted piecemeal, taking up some parts and ignoring others, thus derailing any comprehensive change. Connie McGee, an English language arts supervisor in the Miami/Dade County Public Schools,[2] calls it the key lime pie syndrome. Even though they love the way the whole pie tastes, "they make just the meringue or just the filling and wonder why it doesn't taste like key lime pie."

Also, too often reform efforts focus primarily on administrative organization and structure, leaving the depths of the academic program (and therefore student learning) essentially unchanged.[3] But the schools I've been discussing, the ones that work well, go deep and their focus is primarily on the academic program. The administrators and teachers know the academic program affects what students learn on a daily basis and over time, and they work together to keep it well coordinated and coherent. In this chapter, I'll describe some aspects of the academic program that are markedly different in more effective schools.

In short:

- Support programmatic reviews and expect programmatic changes.
- Ensure that programmatic changes are comprehensive and complete.

THE ACADEMIC PROGRAM WITHIN THE DEPARTMENT

The academic department is such a familiar feature of middle and high school organization that it often gets overlooked in school improvement efforts. Yet it's central in fostering excellence.[4] We all know that there are some superb teachers in almost all schools. Whatever school we went to, most of us remember that wonderful teacher, the one who changed us in a significant way. Those great teachers are important, and we need more of them, but they're not enough. It's the academic program—the built-upon and connected experiences in a subject area across time and across classes—that contributes to learning with a big L, to students' overall literacy and academic development, including their test scores.[5]

When it comes to students' growing ability to read, write, and use language effectively, the English program makes all the difference. Even the best of teachers in more typical schools can provide only isolated moments of excellence and joy for any particular student or group of students in an otherwise disconnected series of English classes. The coherent, coordinated, and well-carried out program is the launching pad for instructional improvement, and this is generally done best at the department level, when the English and language arts faculty act as a disciplinary community. While typical schools may think their programs are coordinated and coherent, too often unintended gaps in skills or content might appear in what gets included from grade to grade, the language used to talk about similar content from class to class or across grades might go unflagged, or connections among parts of the subject taught might seem connected to the teachers but not become apparent to the students. One teacher in a typical school said, "When there's a problem I need to have the students work on or when there's a new material I want to use, I try to stick it in here and there." It is these gaps and "stick ins" that contribute to the lack of content buildup that students experience.

Faculty who have kept up with their academic disciplines in ways I've already described know the potential limitations of tests in their subject area and try to avoid narrowing their departmental curriculum. As they reexamine their programs, they keep excellence within their discipline as their goal. They want their school to have the best English program it can offer, right for their students and right for their field.

Take Parklane,[6] for instance. I've described it in Chapter 2 as a school that treats tests as an opportunity to improve and in Chapter 3 as a great place for professional exchange. It also hones its departmental programs, trying to keep them coherent, challenging, and right for its students. Rachel Kahn's arms are always open, beckoning the English language arts teachers together to improve their program as a whole; they meet and discuss how their students are doing and what else they can do to improve student learning. She sees to it that they act as a departmental team. Such team effort is expected by the school administrators, and the teachers see themselves and their students as benefiting from programmatic unity within their department. The teachers visit each other's classrooms as a way to improve their program, and Rachel visits, too. They see how their work connects with that of the other teachers, and they discuss the curriculum, how it's being carried out, and what their students are experiencing; they also fine-tune the program.

Eija Rougle,[7] the Parklane field researcher, describes it this way: "Parklane's English language arts program forms a kind of organic, malleable whole. It's organic because it's alive, changing, and open ended, yet an integrated structure of parts working together." Although the teachers and their students benefit from the changes that take place in the individual classrooms, it's the departmental program that's the focus. Individual changes are related to something that's cumulative across the department. As they work, Rachel ensures that the state standards and the district curriculum are kept in mind and also that changes are considered in terms of how they'll contribute to students' compounded learning as they move from class to class and grade to grade. Rachel knows how easy it is to take on attractive new materials and ideas, but also how easy it is for these to deflect from the coherent departmental program they're trying to improve. More typical schools, on the other hand, are more likely to take on the latest fads or well-packaged materials without considering how they relate to the program as a whole.

In short:

- Provide departments (or other organizational units) with the authority to review and refine their academic programs to ensure both coherent and coordinated programs.
- Encourage teachers within a department (or grade or team) to review students' academic performance and collaborate in programmatic improvement.
- Ensure content and skill links across grade levels.
- Schedule opportunities for teachers to know what their colleagues are teaching and the approaches they are using.

THE ACADEMIC PROGRAM WITHIN
THE INTERDISCIPLINARY TEAM

In addition to academic departments, many middle and high schools are also divided into interdisciplinary teams such as schools within schools, topically focused academies, or magnet schools.[8] While schools that work well almost always work on program development across subject areas (all of the more effective schools we studied were divided into some sort of interdisciplinary teams[9]), the disciplinary focus and the academic goals that are inherent in the discipline don't get lost, however prevalent the interdisciplinary organization might be.

Let's take International High School,[10] in inner New York City, as an example. It's an unusual school, with entrance limited to students who have been in the United States 4 years or less and who know little English. Students from some 50 countries speak 37 languages, and 84 percent of its students receive free lunches. And students are learning well. Approximately

90 percent of its graduates go on to college. The academic programs are offered in interdisciplinary thematic clusters (motion, for example) of five teachers from the various subject areas and approximately 75 students. Collaboration is a hallmark of the school, and program cohesiveness is the hallmark of each team. The school has a level organizational structure, and the team faculty must assume responsibility for developing and overseeing the effectiveness of their program. Although the teachers plan their program together around a unifying theme, they keep an eye on their disciplines. Each one's subject-area knowledge contributes to students' overall development, and when academic learning in a discipline is not progressing as planned within the program, the team takes action. For example, one team had developed a year-long study of motion, with math, science, social studies, and English taught by the teachers in each discipline. At one point, Marsha S. Slater[11] (who keeps up with her field and is an active English professional in the many ways I've already discussed) began to feel that her students weren't learning particular reading and writing skills well enough. She wanted scheduled time when she could focus explicitly on reading and writing knowledge and skills she thought were essential to the students' learning but not sufficiently captured in their integrated program. She brought this concern to her team that was studying motion and, after much deliberation, they modified the program accordingly.

In comparison, in a more typical high school academy focusing on computers and technology, students had many experiences reading and writing about their coursework—primarily technical articles and manuals. While they occasionally read short stories and novels related to the coursework (e.g., they read *A Clockwork Orange*), students reported dissatisfaction that they had not acquired some knowledge that their age-mates in other programs had because they had not read some of the high school canonical literature; they also wished they were doing more writing. Their literacy performance showed their need as well, but the instructional focus was elsewhere.

In short:

- Even within an interdisciplinary program, ensure that disciplinary knowledge is not lost.

ORGANIZING WHAT GETS TAUGHT: THE BIG PICTURE

Only some academic departments and some teams or academies work well. As you can see, it's not the organizational structure alone that makes the difference, but the scope of thinking and how it's brought together. The program is thought of in a grand sense, as involving the range of what students need to learn, think about, and experience in the subject. There's large-scale orchestration—a shared vision and plan. All parts of the educational system coordinate efforts to make the program work: It's connected, coherent, and rich with content not only on paper but also as it is carried through in action. Teachers and administrators ensure that goals and guidelines are set and followed but also see to it that the curriculum and instructional practices echo, build on, and complement one another across the school year and across the grades. This kind of comprehensiveness is rarely present in typical schools.

Just as in effective businesses, social service agencies, and working environments of other sorts, schools that work well are marked by administrators and teachers who are dedicated to making the larger program work. Teachers know the program well—and thus what other teachers are doing and how the knowledge and skills taught in one grade or during one time of year connect with others. They're able to refer to related lessons and help students become aware of how something they're studying today connects with something else they might have studied last week or last year or with another teacher. It's all part of the big picture the students experience across their day-to-day school lives and across their school years. This requires not only a unity of purpose but also a common overall educational philosophy—a common view of what counts as learning, good performance, and good teaching.

In Miami/Dade County, the English language arts supervisors and teachers have been working for many years to develop and continually refine their program, building a coherent and shared vision of their goals and the professional philosophy that guides their decisions. Sallie Snyder, the English language arts supervisor introduced earlier, says:

> The written guiding principles developed several years ago by the staff reflect our beliefs about what [our program in] language arts/reading instruction entails and includes. These principles continue to serve as a directional compass for our endeavors. The reality is that it is all too easy to get lost in the problems and pressures related to the daily demands for instruction geared toward increased test scores or state-mandated curriculum. This very fact makes necessary and invaluable the existence of a set of guiding principles to which we can return when we begin to feel like we are losing sight of what is truly important and the compass no longer points north.[12]

These principles serve as common ground. They permit the faculty to explore new ways to improve teaching and learning, but to do so in ways that will enhance rather than fragment the already successful program they have established in several schools.[13]

In effective schools, teachers are always involved in the ongoing effort to maintain a coherent but up-to-date academic program. For example, Tawanda Richardson and Alicia Alliston at Charles Drew Middle School[14] in a large California city are part of a review team whose assignment is to see how well their school has integrated the standards into the everyday curriculum and how well their students are doing. But their goal is to examine their program. While they report back to a larger group of teachers from their district, with a focus on larger coordination, they also meet with teachers in their school to discuss their English language arts program, its curriculum, how students and teachers are doing, and what else is needed. At Drew, teacher meetings are used as times when teaching activities and student work are shared, examined, and discussed in light of overall goals and philosophy about what counts and what methods support it. Such ongoing reflection helps to ensure that programmatic coherence is maintained.

Sometimes this coherence is guided by a strong central office administrator who believes in the benefits of programmatic teamwork and who is guided by a vision of whole-program improvement. Take Helen Clark,[15] district English language arts coordinator for a large-city school district in Texas. She knows the difficulty in developing and maintaining a program with common philosophy, guiding principles, and enacted curriculum in a district so large. To maintain programmatic identity as well as curriculum commonality, she calls meetings of the English chairs, the "point person" in each regional cluster, and also two lead teachers in each school. These groups meet on a monthly basis, sometimes together and sometimes with the teachers in their departments, working to develop a common philosophy as well as program and to carry out self-review from that vantage point. In response to statewide standards and testing, Helen and the English faculty have been working hard over several years to develop and fine-tune a comprehensive curriculum guide. But to ensure programmatic coherence, she knows that having a guide is not enough. Teachers need to be involved, to help develop it, know it, and feel comfortable with it and how it works for themselves and for their students.

She says she doesn't want to "create curriculum in a bubble." Therefore, curriculum development is the focus of many meetings within each department as well as across schools. They meet to develop ideas, try them out, give and get feedback; she tries to involve everyone, even in a district of her size, not only once, but over time. So that teachers feel connected to the program, each summer she holds a "summit," where new ideas and strategies are presented and discussed in light of the new curriculum and larger program—and then carried back into the schools for further discussion. With program development in mind, Helen buys professional books for and shares articles with the teachers. She also collaborates with a local university where many of the district's new teachers receive their education. As part of their coursework, prospective teachers use the district curriculum guide and the English language arts program. This is one way new teachers will have a leg up in her program when they are hired. Her goal, she says, is "overall consistency and equity across all schools."

As you can see, in schools that work well, the big picture—program coherence—is paramount. But that coherence isn't born of principles, guidelines, or curriculum materials developed by someone else that teachers are supposed to follow. Too often such projects are coherent on paper but not in action. They end up in a file cabinet, not in teachers' heads, and therefore not in the academic program their students experience. What makes the difference in the higher-performing schools is that the teachers and supervisors together create a coherent program of their own, beyond the standards or guidelines they may have started with. This important instructional development activity permits them to look through a common lens at what others are doing at their school, at what their students are experiencing, and to fix things first hand.

In short:

- Ensure your program is connected and coherent from your students' perspectives, as they experience it over time.
- Keep faculty active in the review and change process, and schedule time for programmatic teamwork.
- Encourage teachers to make overt connections across content, knowledge, and skills—across lessons, classes, and grades.

EXTRA HELP

In this era of tests, many schools offer extra help before, during, and after the regular school day, in Saturday academies, and in summer schools. But what the students experience isn't the same from school to school. In more effective schools, extra help is part of the larger academic program, part of the shared vision and plan and connected to what the students experience in their daily English coursework. Teachers and supervisors meet and discuss what they're doing and how the students are doing; they make connections that add coherence to the students' day and year, and help them improve. When more typical schools offer extra help, and many of them do, these tend to be separate from the curriculum the students experience in their ongoing program. It isn't part of an overall program plan, but rather several disconnected activities.

Take Hudson Middle School,[16] for example. I discussed it briefly in Chapter 3 as a highly collaborative and professionally involved school. It offers remedial reading assistance, but the students are not removed from their classes in order to receive help. Instead, they spend the full day with their regular teachers and have a tutorial time at the end of the day, when students return to their teams. At that time, students needing remedial reading meet with the reading teachers, and students with special needs work with their special education teachers. But these teachers stay in close touch; if a team teacher feels a student needs extra help and wants to work with that student on his or her particular coursework, it's arranged.

Because the reading teachers are part of the English language arts department, they attend department meetings. They also attend team meetings and parent conferences. And they keep in touch about ways to help the students within the English language arts program. For example, Cathy Starr, the Hudson middle grade teacher, talks with the reading teacher before beginning each major assignment. They discuss goals for the assignment, difficulties students might encounter, and strategies they'll work on that students need to learn. They then focus on the same material in both time slots (English class and end-of-day extra help) if they feel it will help the students. Starr says, "This gives them double support."

Hudson also has a Strive for Success evening tutorial project where parents and students learn to work together on study skills and strategies that are related to what the students are learning in class. The teachers of the students write brief weekly reports for the teachers and aides working in Strive for Success, who discuss the reports among themselves and also with the classroom teachers. Then appropriate activities are developed for the parents and their children to do together. Coordination continues.

Hudson is a mainstreamed school, which means that students who have special physical, emotional, or intellectual needs attend regular rather than special education classes. A few such students are in almost every class. As in many schools, an individual educational plan is developed by a special education teacher for each student with special needs. This is discussed at meetings attended by all relevant teachers, as well as parents and caretakers, and is carried out within the regular academic program. Students are taught the same curriculum as everyone else, and teaching assistants help them during regular class time. Along with the subject teachers and reading teachers, teaching assistants and special education teachers are part of each instructional team. They work with all subject teachers their students see, and they help each student stay connected to each ongoing academic program. They're linchpins connecting the regular curriculum with special learning needs. The teaching assistants attend team meetings and all parent conferences where their students are involved. The special education teacher attends team meetings when possible, and the house principal and guidance counselor attend weekly. Because the team shares a daily common planning time, extra meetings are called when needed, and informal catch-ups about lessons and how students are doing are common.

These informal catch-ups extend to students, too. Many teachers open their classroom doors early and their students arrive for help—with homework or with questions about readings, projects, or what they have recently studied in class. Starr says, "It isn't official, just something we do. The same for after school. We have an activity period 3 days a week from 3:25 to 4:05. In addition to the end-of-day tutorial, all teachers are available then for extra help. That includes remedial reading and special education teachers." All this is part of the teachers' commitment to carry their academic program through to student learning.

In comparison, in one typical school two separate private companies were given contracts to help improve scores; one offered tutorial help to the students after school while the other offered instructional improvement workshops for teachers, with lessons to follow in class. But these two groups had very different approaches and never spoke to each other. In addition, classes were offered on Saturday by school and district teachers who responded to a call for additional work. They never met with the classroom teachers of the students or with each other. The special education programs in this school are also separate, with almost no exchange with teachers in the regular program.

In excellent schools, the extra attention is not limited to students who are having difficulty but is offered to all students, including those who are advanced and talented learners. Parklane, for example, offers enrichment clubs of all sorts, including a science club for girls that is sponsored in collaboration with a local university and others that focus on students' interests and talents in the academic subjects, the arts, and related areas. A Writers in the Schools program provides opportunities for students to be motivated by, work with, and receive feedback from working writers. These activities are in addition to a more formal advanced curriculum that is offered to higher-performing students for "enrichment." Hudson has a teacher whose responsibility is to provide enrichment activities to students. Her class content is flexible, changing based on the talents of the students (e.g., writing, drama, art, music, scientific inquiry). In addition, advanced (high school) courses are offered in math, science, and art. The music program has many offerings and draws many students into vocal and instrumental classes. The enrichment programs often extend beyond the schoolday, both before and after regular class hours. While typical schools may try to offer enrichment, it is low on their list of priorities: "We just don't have the time. We've got to get the test scores up."

In short:

- Keep extra help relevant to the students' ongoing program.
- Provide time for extra help and regular program teachers to discuss course content, approaches, and students' needs.
- Provide special offerings for all students, including gifted and talented students, and activities to spark special interests.

ACADEMIC PROGRAMS IN EFFECTIVE SCHOOLS: HOW THEY WORK

Overall, the more effective schools have coordinated, connected, and comprehensive programs. They know that lone excellent teachers create memorable experiences for students but don't raise scores or create truly higher-performing students. Students need rich and coherent programs carried into extended, engaging instructional experiences throughout their school careers. In comparison, the more typical schools don't believe they have time for looking at the big picture and for building connections. Nor do they think a cohesive pedagogical theory of teaching and learning and a coherent departmental program to carry it through are critical to students' success. They buy the old assumption that what goes on behind the classroom door is each teacher's responsibility, rather than a critical part of a larger academic program. In schools that work well there's a grand plan, a whole pie. The teachers know it; the students feel it. The programs work.

Now, rate your school, using the chart on the next page.

How Effective Is Your School?—Academics

		RATE YOUR SCHOOL		
MORE EFFECTIVE SCHOOLS:	*LESS EFFECTIVE SCHOOLS:*	Doing Well	Needs Improvement	Needs to Get Started
Assume change in the academic program is normal and desirable.	Assume change in the academic program is needed only if problems arise.			
Expect the development and carrying through of a coherent program.	May produce coherence on paper, but not in practice.			
Provide time for teachers to learn what others are teaching—and how.	Expect teachers to follow the written curriculum and instructional materials, but no more.			
See this course (or year) in relation to the larger academic program.	See the course being taught as an entity in and of itself.			
Encourage faculty to help their students see how the parts fit and relate over time.	Focus on the lesson goals but do not make overt connections to other lessons or courses.			
Maintain open communication between regular and extra-help teachers and relatedness in what the students experience.	Adopt several extra-help offerings with no communication among teachers and unrelated to the regular program or each other.			
Provide extra offerings to spark interest and enrichment as well as to help.	Offer extra help but not enrichment.			

Instruction Aims High and
Is Responsive to Students

OF COURSE THE BEST planned and most seamlessly coordinated program doesn't work unless instruction is carried out in ways that make a difference in what and how students learn.[1] In schools that work well, the focus on improved instruction is paramount. As I described in Chapter 4, there is a common theoretical approach to student learning and to teaching that guides the kinds of instructional changes that are made, leaving little room for fads or quick fixes. So, even in an era when one instructional approach is pitted against another as the "right" or "best" way to teach, decisions in these schools are anchored in the reality of the classroom, what works best on a day-to-day basis for students of the particular school. Overall, instruction in the schools that work well occurs in what I have come to call "envisionment-building" classes.[2] Envisionments are what you understand and think about at any point in time; they are the understandings, questions, hunches and momentary ideas that are in our minds as we build understandings—across subject areas and experiences.[3] For example, at this point in your reading of the book, your envisionment might include some ideas about the kind of effective schools I've been describing and how they work, and you likely have ideas about how your own school is similar or different. But you probably also have questions about things I haven't discussed yet, questions about those I have, and perhaps some ideas you think might fit and some disagreements, too. This is a normal part of the coming-to-understand process. In envisionment-building classes, teachers engage students in the kinds of thought-provoking experiences that provide them with an opportunity to inspect new ideas and skills, try them out, question, explore, and use them in ways that substantively add to their available knowledge base. They provide opportunities for students' envisionments to grow—for deeper, more elaborated understandings to develop. The instructional challenge is to help envisionment-building move along—to become more refined, better elaborated, better connected, and more useful in new situations. More typical instruction stops earlier in the learning process when the ideas are less well developed, inhibiting the potential for richer understandings.

In short:

- Shape instruction to your students' realities, abilities, and needs.
- Invite questions, suppositions, and momentary ideas as part of the process of acquiring new knowledge; use them as points of discussion and examination.
- Aim for an envisionment-building classroom.

AIMING HIGH

Students are shortchanged when the goal of instruction is simply for them to get the right answer. Too often lessons end just because students have given this answer—said it, chosen it, or written it. In this situation, the trick for students (what they consider their goal) is to guess what the teacher wants; and even when they get an answer right, they aren't always sure why. Many of us remember studying that way, attending more to getting the answer our teacher wanted than to whether we understood what it was all about or whether we could do it again.

Student learning is enhanced, on the other hand, when the goal of instruction is to build a network of concepts and an understanding of how to use them. In this case, teachers don't stop teaching just because the material is covered and students have reached particular achievement goals. Instead, they treat "getting it" as the groundwork from which to help students reach deeper and more connected understandings. As a matter of course, students are expected to build rich envisionments—to go beyond giving definitions and explanations and to be able to engage in analyses and critiques, to conduct research, or to imagine possible applications or effects. Even the lowest-performing students are taught to think and discuss and write about new ideas in ways that clarify their understandings and make them better learners. I call this a focus on "generative learning." It happens when students are taught ways to go beyond recognition or recitation, to understand and reason about and with difficult knowledge and skills, and to use them in new ways. Generative learning is the goal of instruction we see in schools that work well. They're after higher stakes than the high-stakes tests call for.

Let's take Suzanna Matton's twelfth-grade class in Springfield High School[4] as an example. I introduced Suzanna and her school in Chapter 3. Springfield High is a large school with 2,500 students in a large city in California. Sixty-three percent of its students are Hispanic, 15 percent White, 10 percent African American, and 9 percent Asian. Thirty-three languages are spoken at home. It's a highly successful school. It has high Advanced Placement course scores based on nationwide standards, its SAT scores are above the district average in English and math, and in 1998 it was rated as one of the top three schools in the city by a widely read newspaper. Local colleges come to the school to recruit and leave literature and announcements in the classrooms. On Matton's classroom wall is a sign: "You never fail until you stop trying." And she always goes for generative learning.

When her twelfth-grade students read *Waiting for Godot*, she helped them build rich envisionments. They took turns reading it, discussed the play act by act, and engaged in various related activities to understand it better. They did what they needed to develop a general understanding of the play, and typical teachers would stop here. But Matton aims much higher for her students. She went on to have her students elaborate their envisionments by taking the perspectives of characters in the play, discussing their perceptions of other characters, and comparing them. Then she helped them think about what the characters represented. They discussed symbolism. They also looked for parallels between the characters in the play and how we live as characters in the play of life. At this point she recounted some of the history of the play and discussed Samuel Beckett as a writer, the Theater of the Absurd, and existential thought. With this background, the class discussed how these themes were echoed in *Waiting for Godot* and how knowing about them affected their interpretation of the play. Then they made comparisons to other works and authors. In the end, the students had not only learned about the play, and about literary traditions and history, but had also learned new content that gave them alternative ways to interpret; they had gained new, high literacy skills. And the students stayed engaged and loved it.

Some might say that what happens in Matton's class is fine for a good senior class, but what about students who are having real problems at school? Celeste Rotundi[5] also teaches at Springfield, in the Bilingual Business and Finance Academy. This is a program for students at risk for dropping out of high school. The academy offers the regular academic program combined with a career path that utilizes bilingual skills. For her eleventh-grade class, she created a unit on affirmative action and debate, where she had her students read one book or article advocating affirmative action and another against. They built envisionments by discussing both and their reactions to the two. Having covered the material, this would be the stopping point in many typical classrooms.

But in her classroom, this was just the starting point. She went on to help them build richer envisionments. Next, students analyzed and learned ways to structure an argument (needed for their statewide writing test) as well as to work through their ideas related to civil rights. They wrote argumentative papers from their own perspectives. Then she assigned students a persona with views different from their own and asked them to give brief speeches from that perspective. Discussions and counterarguments followed, along with analyses of current issues. Rotundi's lesson could have stopped after they had read and discussed both sides of the debate on affirmative action. Instead, she went further, offering a variety of reading, writing, and oral experiences with argumentative structures in ways students could begin to internalize and use in new situations. She gave these "at-risk" students the tools to refine or rethink their own views as they dealt with opinions and arguments with which they were unfamiliar. She helped them build networks of ideas that will be useful to them in life as well as in class.

Typical schools, in comparison, leave little time for this rich development of ideas. In fact, they rarely leave time for discussion. One teacher said, "If I allow discussion, there won't be time to cover everything. Besides, my students don't know enough to get into a discussion. So I feel I need to tell them everything." In her class, she leads her students through each lesson as laid out in the textbook. They read together, answer the questions together, then move on. They don't even do the text's follow-up activities: "There's no time."

In short:

- Aim to help students build a network of concepts and understandings, and to use them in new contexts.
- Leave time to help students clarify their understandings.
- Encourage "minds on" the topic through engaging activities (e.g., critiques, research, predicting effects and outcomes).
- Guide students to examine alternatives, form their own perspectives, and develop well-founded arguments about issues they are learning.
- Aim for generative learning, where students are challenged to use skills and knowledge in new ways.
- Help students connect what they are learning to larger issues in the discipline, their lives, and the world.

TEACHING STUDENTS WHAT TO DO

When we think of instruction, most of us think about the content that's to be learned. And, as you know from your own experience as well as from my examples of Matton's and Rotundi's classrooms, of course content is important. But in learning, there are also strategies, ways to go about thinking or ways to go about doing things, that are also important. At home and in society there's a long tradition of teaching strategies. Parents and caretakers do this when they demonstrate how to ride a bike or how to follow a recipe. The content matters, but what to do first, next, and last and what to focus on when are also critical. Schools that work well teach students strategies for thinking about and using the content they study. Envisionment-building is involved here, too, as students develop deeper understandings, a mind-set for how to get the job done.

Strategies are taught in many ways. Teachers segment difficult tasks and show students how to go about doing them (or thinking about them), a bit at a time. This part of learning is like an apprenticeship, where teachers guide students through the process and teach the steps necessary to do well. They discuss, model, and practice the strategies; they offer guides and prompts, and they give reminders. Over time, students internalize ways to understand what certain tasks call for, how to see them through, how to evaluate what they've done, and what they can do to make their performance better.

For an example of effective strategy instruction, let's look at Kate McFadden-Midby's middle school class at Foshay Learning Center[6] in Los Angeles. I mentioned it in Chapter 2. It's in an inner-city school in a high-poverty area. Sixty-nine percent of the students are Hispanic, 31 percent African American, and 86 percent of them receive free lunches. In 1989, when Howard Lappin became principal, it was the lowest-scoring school in Los Angeles. He restructured the school by making it a K–12 school, with a focus on instruction. In addition to the regular high school, he added an academically oriented college prep magnet program. It's primarily a neighborhood school and has all the effective qualities I've described in the previous chapters. Throughout the year, McFadden-Midby teaches her students both strategies to think about the material they're learning and strategies to complete the tasks successfully.

At one point she felt her students needed to become more aware of how to use and reflect on order and sequence in their reading, writing, and other coursework. After discussing and analyzing how temporal and spatial order were evident in the literature they had read, students focused on how to create a well-structured paper, listed its features, and wrote papers that incorporated order or sequence. One of their learning activities involved ranking people's qualities (most to least), time sequence (first to last), and popularity (highest to lowest). They needed to list the critical points for each and then find language to discuss them. Another time, they were asked to remember and then discuss activities they had engaged in recently where order was important and to write an essay about it, using the organizational and language strategies they had learned. They reviewed the way time-sequence papers could be organized, reviewed the critical information that should be present, and developed a set of criteria to judge a good paper. They used these criteria to review and redraft their papers, using the strategies they had learned.

McFadden-Midby offers such strategy help throughout the year: developing reading and writing guides with her students, giving them suggestions about the kinds of issues they need to think about, and providing them lists of things to do or include as well as the qualities that good work of a particular sort includes. These strategies help the students build envisionments for how to do well at the moment and also give them useful tools that they will be able to use in understanding the demands of other tasks.

In more typical schools, on the other hand, the focus is primarily on content—on whether students have gotten the right answer rather than on how to get to the answer, or on how to organize the paper but not necessarily how to go about thinking through what they are going to write. When strategies are offered, they generally involve handouts of formats for students to follow, primarily when writing. But these are rarely taught in a way that helps students build envisionments of the task replete with strategies to organize their thoughts and actions; they are simply templates to follow.

In short:

- Teach students strategies for how to think about as well as how to carry through assignments and activities.
- Offer instructional apprenticeships—with models, guides, prompts, reminders, and other helpful support.
- Teach students strategies for how to judge their understandings as well as the effectiveness of the work they do.

TEACHING SKILLS

Most of us remember the ways we were taught English skills. Some of us wince at the memory of our struggles with vocabulary, grammar, or poetic devices. One of two approaches was probably used. Some of us received primarily a skills-based approach: We were taught rules, meanings, and procedures; memorized and practiced them; and then were tested on what we remembered. Job done. Others of us were taught primarily by an experience-based approach: New skills and knowledge were encountered in the course of assigned reading and writing activities. In this case teachers would help us do a good job on the activities, but the underlying rules, meanings, and procedures were rarely made overt. The way we were taught has as much to do with our age as the school we went to. In the field of education, there has been a long-standing debate about the effectiveness of skills-based and experience-based instruction, at least throughout the entire 20th century and on into the 21st.

Despite the debate, teachers in schools that work well use their students as their guide. They read and keep up with the debate, but what works for their students is what they use. And without doubt, they use a variety of approaches to instruction, based on student needs, state standards, the faculty-developed curriculum, and their shared vision for high literacy.[7] Teachers use a mix of skills-based and experience-based instruction when appropriate, and students work in groups, as a whole class, and alone when appropriate. What matters is that the activities are selected to provide students with "minds-on" and connected envisionment-building experiences that are engaging, challenging, and lead to new learnings.

There are three kinds of activities that effective teachers use to help students learn new skills, and they use them flexibly as needed. They're not unlike the varied kinds of helpful experiences parents and caretakers offer to young children who are first learning the complexities of their mother tongue—how it works and how to use it to their advantage. I call them separated, simulated, and integrated activities.[8]

If students need to learn a particular skill, concept, or rule, teachers might separate it—point it out, tell what it means and how it works, and highlight its particular features. This helps students become aware of what an item looks like, means, or connotes. With toddlers or schoolchildren, separated activities help learners focus on particular aspects of language, literacy, and concepts; they highlight the critical features. It's like when parents say and stress the word *ran*—"The dog just *ran*. I just *ran*. And you *ran*, too"—when they want the child to focus on the correct past tense form *ran* instead of saying *runned* (as all young children do when they overgeneralize using *-ed* for the past tense[9]).

In school, teachers might say, "People do persuasive writing when they want to convince other people to think in a particular way or to do something. So, when you do persuasive writing, you need to tell what you want the person to do or how to think and why it's important to do so. Think for a moment about some times when you tried to persuade someone to do something that was important to you—maybe a parent or a friend. Jot down two or three persuasions that come to mind. When you're done, meet in groups to discuss your persuasions and together choose one that you think worked best. Use these questions to help guide your choice: (1) Who was the audience? (2) What was the goal? (3) What was most persuasive? Why? (4) How did the person deal with objections either before or after they came up?" Each group would present their chosen "persuasion" and explain why they thought it was effective, followed by discussion about "what works." This would help move their envisionments of persuasion along, refining their judgments about criteria to use in planning a persuasive encounter and also in writing a persuasive paper. The next day the students could be reminded of their work the previous day and then be asked to write a persuasive paper about a given topic. But before beginning, they could be given a list of questions to guide their persuasive writing. It might look like this: (1) Who is my audience? (2) What do I want them to do or think? (3) What arguments will sway them to my side? (4) What objections do I think they'll have that I'll need to counter? (5) Why is it important for them to think or act in the way I'd like? After answering any questions the students might have, the teacher might then say, "Write these questions down so you can use them for reference." Students could use the question as the basis for a discussion in class that day and a guide as they write their persuasive papers that day and in the future.

Separated activities differ from simulated activities, whose primary purpose is to give students practice using a skill or concept that they'll build upon in the future. When parents and teachers use a simulated approach, they help learners become comfortable in using a new skill. Parents do this when they say, "Let's tell about everything we did yesterday." In responding to this, the child would be practicing past tense forms.

Situated approaches in the classroom often look like practice (e.g., "Now it's your turn to . . ."). To help students build envisionments of how to write effective persuasions, teachers might say, "Look at this persuasive essay and this persuasive letter. In the pieces you've just read, how do you know the authors were trying to persuade someone?" This would lead students into a discussion of word choice and organization as well as the underlying rules of persuasive writing—which they would then practice as they write their own persuasive piece.

Separated and simulated activities differ from each other and from integrated activities, where knowledge and skills are called on in the course of ongoing activities. Here students rely on their envisionments to decide what is called for in the particular situation as well as how to use it within the particular larger activity in which they are engaged. At home integrated activities happen when children talk to others, play make-believe, or write letters to grandma about what they've done. Past tense is needed, but the message leading to the desired outcome, not the tense, is the goal. It takes knowledge of the tense to do these real things well, but sometimes more help is needed to learn to be effective in the particular situation.

At school, students engage in many activities that integrate all of their language and literacy skills, whether doing a research project or writing about a civic problem. To complete the activity effectively, students need fairly well-developed envisionments; they need to use their knowledge and skills pertaining to persuasive as well as other forms of writing, but getting the full job done well—the ideas presented and their likely effectiveness—is the goal. Here, again, form and skill count but are not enough. Students also need to decide what content and presentation are appropriate and will work well. If they need help, parents and teachers both might offer separated or simulated experiences using the words or ideas in another context, reminding them of a rule, or practicing it, but they will also help them make judgments and take action—they will discuss how it fits within the larger activity and how to use it effectively.

Although all three approaches to learning new skills are common at home and in classes that work well, they don't happen in all schools. They certainly didn't epitomize the kinds of instruction many of us remember. Although we likely were taught primarily by a skills-based or an experienced-based approach, neither alone seems to do the job as well as one that responds flexibly to students' needs.

In typical schools one approach predominates, almost to the exclusion of the others. For example, in one high school the focus was on the language, grammar, and usage practice the school felt the students needed. Exercise materials (e.g., workbooks, overhead transparency sets, grammar books) were ordered for each class. For language practice, for example, students would copy analogies and antonyms from the overhead projector, circle the correct response, then write a dictionary definition. For grammar practice, the teacher would read the explanations and examples given at the beginning of each exercise, model the procedure on the first sentence, and then the students would copy the sentences from the book for correction. Although the purchased materials could have been used within a more comprehensive approach to skills learning, instead they became the foundation for a curriculum of separated skills activities. And because there was little concern with providing related simulated and integrated activities, students had little opportunity to build fuller envisionments of how to use the skills at work.

In short:

- Use a variety of instructional approaches flexibly, based on students' learning needs; don't rely excessively on one approach.
- Whatever the instructional approach, allow students ample opportunity to try things out, ask questions, receive help, and judge their own performance.

IMPROVED INSTRUCTION

As you can see, the best-developed program won't work without its symbiotic partner—well-developed, challenging, and helpful envisionment-building instruction. There are a depth, quality, and responsiveness to students' instructional needs that differentiate more effective from more typical schools. Instruction aims beyond the content to deeper and more generative learning. It helps students gain real expertise by teaching them strategies for how to do things and how to use ideas in new as well as known situations. It offers multiple kinds of support and experiences to ensure students will learn the skills and knowledge that provide the foundation for their growing expertise. And it's flexible, responsive to the particular students and their particular needs in their particular situation. All this, and the basics are getting covered as well, in a range of lessons and activities, with a range of useful practice. But it takes a knowledgeable professional faculty to become familiar with what particular instruction to offer to students, how to know when each is needed or not, and what is most helpful to which students and when. This is where everything the schools that work do comes into play, supporting professional growth for teachers and academic growth for students.

Now, rate your school, using the chart on the next page.

How Effective Is Your School?—Instruction

		RATE YOUR SCHOOL		
MORE EFFECTIVE SCHOOLS:	**LESS EFFECTIVE SCHOOLS:**	Doing Well	Needs Improvement	Needs to Get Started
Treat learning as a process of questioning, trying out, and grappling with new ideas and skills.	Treat learning as adhering one bit of knowledge to another.			
Aim to teach students a network of understandings, to connect and use in new ways.	Aim to teach students the content within the confines of the lesson.			
Treat "getting it" as groundwork to teach deeper understandings.	Treat "getting it" as a lesson done.			
Help students relate new learning to larger issues in the discipline and the world.	Help students learn the content but not how to relate it to larger issues.			
Use writing, discussion, drama, and art as opportunities to engage students in thinking through the new ideas.	Consider discussion, drama, art, and writing (apart from writing instruction) as time away from content learning.			
Teach strategies for ways to think about and use the content in assignments and activities.	Teach new content but not strategies for thinking about or using it.			
Aim to deliver substantive and engaged learning experiences.	Aim to cover the content.			
Use separated, simulated, and integrated instructional approaches flexibly, in response to students' needs.	Use one primary instructional approach.			

Parents, Community, and Schools
Work Together—Really

As I MENTIONED in the last chapter, the particular school situation—who the students are and what they need—counts a great deal and schools that work well extend beyond their doors. Most of us know that schools feel good and work better when parents and the community are involved. Common sense and our own experience tell us this, and research bears it out. In schools that work well, parents and community are in the picture, not peripheral, as they tend to be in typical schools. Parents feel as if they know what their children are experiencing and what's being planned, have a voice in what's happening, and have someone who will help them with problems. Local businesses, civic groups, and residents consider the school a central part of their community, want it to work well, and feel part of the effort. Successful schools elevate the reputation of the community, potentially to everyone's benefit. For their part, schools find it's to their advantage to open their doors to the community and involve residents in school-sponsored activities, problem solving, plans, and decisions. Everyone benefits. A number of years ago, Lisa Delpit[1] wrote a book called *Other People's Children*. It's a good book, and I particularly like the title. It reminds us that family and community lives are at the core of who children are and that for students to do well at school, their home and community experiences, values, and goals need to be understood and honored. Successful schools know this and seek involvement. The stakeholders—educators, parents, and community members—work toward their common goal of the well-educated child in ways that work for them and their locality.

Schools that work are part of the community. They involve their constituency in running the school and in maintaining high standards, and they also make the school a resource for the community. This chapter describes several important kinds of involvement, using two schools—a middle and high school—as examples. Both are successful in their degree of outreach and involvement, but the communities are very different.

In short:

- Involve parents and community members as partners in running the school and maintaining high standards.
- Understand the community's educational experiences, goals, and needs.

SCHOOL MANAGEMENT

Most of us are members of a number of organizations, be they civic, religious, cultural, or social. Almost all reach out to their constituents and try to involve them in some way. But we know that there's involvement and then there's *involvement*, and they're not the same. Too often we're asked to work on committees, help out at functions, and raise money. But we're not involved in deciding what the groups do or how they should change. Even as supporters, we sometimes disagree with things that are happening but have no forum for discussion. Sometimes we suspect things are happening that we don't know about but want to. We feel out of the loop, and it makes us distrustful. The same is true in relation to schools, but in a way that involves much more anxiety: Our children are at stake. More successful schools work hard to create mechanisms for substantive parent and community involvement, while in typical schools they hardly exist.

As in business, school-based management is a well-researched concept that involves all stakeholders in decision making: teachers, administrators, parents, community members, and sometimes even students. They work on committees that deal with everything from academics to upkeep. Take Springfield High School,[2] for example. I described it in a fair amount of detail in Chapters 3 and 5. It's adopted a school-based management approach, and this leadership mechanism provides a vehicle for parents and teachers to stay actively involved in shaping and maintaining the school. The principal expects and welcomes input into decision making and says, "Dissenting voices can be heard." He believes in "action through group planning." Several committees, from finance to academics, work in conjunction with a school-based governance council that has representation from the various stakeholder groups. The governance council tries to keep in touch with the community at large and to be responsive to what it hears. At one point it developed a Parent Needs Assessment Survey to determine what parents wanted to know about programs, as well as concerns they had, and used the feedback in planning. It also decided to apply for Western Accreditation, which necessitates a self-study that it wanted to do anyway. All in all, quite a number of committees meet separately to study, learn, and make recommendations. Support is high, as are parent satisfaction ratings.

You may say that Springfield is an urban school with potential problems and that's why it tries so hard to build bridges. But, in fact, substantive parent and community involvement is usual in almost all schools that work well. Henry Hudson Middle School[3] (discussed in Chapters 3 and 4) is located in a suburban community in upstate New York with a homogeneous middle-class student body. Academic achievement has a high priority, test scores are consistently high, and everyone works hard to maintain the school's excellence. Its reputation is a draw for home buyers with school-age children. Here, too, parent and community involvement is an integral part of district policy.[4]

Hudson's districtwide school-based management team was formed before any formal state requirements were developed. (Since the early 1990s, New York State mandates that every school have a shared decision-making plan[5] that includes a site-based management group with parents.) The PTA is responsible for appointing parent members, teacher members are elected, and administrators take turns serving 2-year terms. There is a districtwide set of committees and also Building Cabinets and working groups at each school. Districtwide committees include Shared Decision-Making, Review of District Policy, Citizens' Budget Committee, District Priorities Committee, Safe and Drug-Free Schools Advisory Committee, Emergency Response, and districtwide Technology Planning Committee. When committees are formed, an announcement appears in a newsletter or mailing to the entire community, inviting volunteers.

The Building Cabinet is responsible for establishing school goals and priorities, plans and processes to achieve them, and monitoring results. It also reviews school budget proposals, facilitates parent involvement on other building teams, and recommends and supports a range of curriculum offerings, assessment practices, and administrative procedures. When Hudson set up its Building Cabinet, it initially involved a committee of teachers and administrators but soon expanded to include teaching assistants and parents. Students now also participate. While the building principal and one or two other administrators are Cabinet members, teachers and parents outnumber them. Administrators never chair the Cabinet. Meetings are open, and the agenda is available before the meeting. Staff members and parents attend, express concerns, and offer views. The Cabinet meets one day a month (sometimes two half-days), and substitutes are hired to take over the teachers' classes during meeting time.

Parents also serve on other school committees. For example Cathy Starr,[6] the Hudson teacher mentioned in Chapters 3 and 4, chaired the building technology committee for a number of years and looked to parents with special knowledge as active committee members. Guided by a parent who knew more about computers than the other members of the committee, it studied school needs and drew up a plan for projected uses and purchases, including wiring the building for Internet access. Another committee of teachers, parents, and administrators revised the "Language Arts Expectations" document that specifies expected student performance. And when Hudson searched for a new principal, parents, teachers, teaching assistants, and custodians sat on the committee.

Beyond the school, there is also a districtwide Technology Planning Committee (as well as other committees) where parents play similarly important roles and impact decisions. Parents, community members, and district employees also serve on the district's annual Citizens' Budget Committee. It develops the budget that's presented to the district each spring. The district believes that all stakeholders who will be affected by the action should be included in the decision. This is a far cry from more typical schools, where parent involvement in school management is almost nonexistent: "They just don't show up, except for the special interests and the troublemakers." They haven't done the groundwork to develop trusting and respectful partnerships.

In short:

- Substantively involve parents and community members in school management, planning, and decision making.

- Actively engage parents and community members on the range of school committees—from academics to upkeep, from problem solving to dreaming.
- Build collaborative bridges as a way to solve problems.
- Tap parents' and community members' expertise as a way to enhance school management.
- Do the groundwork to make parents and community members feel comfortable and know you need them.

CHILDREN'S SCHOOL LIVES

In schools that work well, everyone is also directly involved in children's school lives; they work together and offer support. Parents and community members are not merely informed about school programs and offerings but get involved in how they work. At Springfield, for example, parent involvement is integral and ongoing—and generates real understandings and helpful suggestions on the parents' part. The school sends home course planning materials before the beginning of each semester, and parents must approve the courses their children take. Someone at school is available to help them. Once students are enrolled, parents are kept up to date on how each child is doing with performance reports or report cards sent home about every five weeks.

In addition to a parents' night each semester, parents are encouraged to request a conference with the teachers and regularly do so. When students have difficulties of any sort, parents are called in to discuss the matter and, when appropriate, assistance is given to help both them and the teacher follow through. Parents are invited to set up appointments to discuss their children's courses or programs, and their questions, feedback, and involvement are welcome. A support group comprised of both local counseling services and school staff is available for students and families who need help with such things as parenting; anger, crisis, sobriety, and grief management; and tobacco education. Springfield believes addressing students' non-academic needs can have a substantial impact on both academic and personal growth.

Hudson helps students and their families, too. It's a particularly supportive and collegial school where parents have always been welcome; no one can remember a time when it was otherwise. The school aims to know its students well and to develop working relationships with parents.

Teachers and administrators believe that students do better when assigned to classes in smaller units (or houses) where students and teachers work together and know each other well. Therefore, Hudson's administration includes one building principal and three house principals, one for each house. Each house principal is responsible for about 500 students. Since the students stay in the same house all 3 years, the principals and teachers really get to know the students and families. It isn't unusual for a parent with a concern to stop in for a chat, often calling the principal by first name. They're welcome and are expected to make contact whenever they have a concern or question. They're also invited to sit in on meetings when their child is being discussed. In addition to their participation during this meeting, discussion with the teacher usually precedes and follows the visit.

Report cards are issued once every 10 weeks, but interim reports are also sent home for each student at the midpoint of each marking period. Therefore, as in Springfield, parents and caretakers receive an update every 5 weeks, keeping them apprised of their child's work, progress, and needs. Parent phone calls are expected and routine, and parents and teachers also stay in touch via e-mail.

Teachers work together in teams responsible for the same group of students. When a student's behavior changes, the team discusses that child during their daily planning time and often calls the parent and follows up with a parent–school team conference. The house principal, counselor, and special education teacher meet weekly with each team so they can work together; they attend parent conferences when appropriate. There are usually between one and three parent conferences every week, with all team members in attendance. The teaching teams generally also have some kind of weekly contact with parents whose children are having difficulty, either by phone, note, or e-mail. Sometimes a weekly report is sent home to help parents, teachers, and students work together. The report includes comments from all of that student's teachers.

Each team has its own special activities for parents, such as having a tea during American Education Week, when parents are invited not just to sit in on classes but also to join their children in the cafeteria for lunch. Parents are, of course, invited (and needed) on all field trips, large and small. Hudson also has team newsletters. And some teams participate in a school information line organized by a local newspaper. Teachers call and record a weekly message describing the class work, giving dates for assignments and suggesting outside reading. Reminders of these numbers are always in the team newsletters.

The school also has a newsletter that goes home with each report card and informs parents of important whole-school activities. In addition, the district uses the local cable access channel; school board meetings and speakers are always televised, and cable TV is used to inform parents and community members of school activities. An open house is held at the beginning of each school year, usually within the first 3 weeks. The Building Cabinet is very active in designing and redesigning this. There are evaluation forms for parents and for teachers at the end of the evening, and they are used to make changes for the next year.

While typical schools also have back-to-school night, parent meetings, and other activities designed to report to parents about their children's school lives, too often these are planned and run by school personnel who tell parents about programs, changes, expectations, and what they can do to help, with little parent understanding of the issues at hand, input into the changes, or invitation to become involved in any way. One typical school principal, for example, maintained an extremely friendly relationship with the parents and encouraged her teachers to do so. They had potluck dinners at school where everyone was friendly. These were times when the faculty would tell the parents about the new test requirements and school changes such as a dress code and the need to sign off on homework. But parents were never asked to become involved in school management of any sort, not in the ways the effective schools did.

In short:

- Involve parents and community members in children's school lives, including curriculum, instruction, and assessment.
- Keep parents frequently apprised of how their children are doing, with explanations about needed help, enrichment, or other needs.
- Know the students and work with parents to head off problems before they escalate.
- Maintain a communication system—paper or technology based— that keeps parents informed about homework and class work as well as changes in school routines.

SCHOOL OFFERINGS WITHIN AND BEYOND THE SCHOOL

Schools that work well reach out to students with a wide range of offerings, and parents are involved. At Springfield, parents and community members sit on planning and advisory committees, and several community-based organizations and businesses contribute to the curriculum offerings through mentoring, internships, training courses, and special offerings both at school and in the community. The school wants to engage students in challenging academics but also wants to help them think about and prepare for what they will do when they leave school.

In addition to its regular program, Springfield has instituted academies and magnet programs that help students become familiar with various professions and give them specific strengths for college or work. For example, an international business and language program focuses on the world, dealing with global aspects of economics, culture, transportation, and business. Beyond their regular academic coursework, which includes Advanced Placement courses, students take at least one foreign-language course each year. A bilingual business academy was developed for students with low scores, preparing them for eventual careers in business, with a focus on the uses of bilingual skills in world trade and international affairs. A technology academy offers hands-on learning about and with technology across all subjects. All offer academically challenging programs. More important, each of these programs was developed based on strengths in the community and is tightly tied to the community. Parents are helped to understand how the programs work and to make decisions about their children's choices.

Community corporations, businesses, and civic groups play an active role. In these programs, students are matched with mentors from the community based on personal interests, academic needs, and career objectives. The mentors stay in frequent touch with the students, discuss coursework, tutor, offer enrichment, and help students find post–high school possibilities. In addition, local corporations, businesses, radio stations, and performing arts groups supply equipment, create Internet hookups, help with performances and arts programs, fund programs, and arrange for students to have internships. Several organizations target specific ethnic groups (e.g., African American, Hispanic) and offer special opportunities for academic, financial, and cultural support.

The local colleges and university are also involved. Springfield has tried to develop a "college culture," providing all students with a college preparatory curriculum, academic support, and many experiences in and with college faculty and students. Students can take some courses in local colleges for high school and college credit. And a program is in place to help students as early as middle school begin to prepare for college.

Springfield also has a community service program. Each student must spend 48 hours working in the community. Students help in the local nursing homes and community center, assist with reading programs at the library, and work in the town's parks and recreational programs. Teachers and community members work together to ensure that it's a learning experience for the students as well as a benefit to the community.

Hudson's parents and community are also involved in school offerings. For example, a funded program for students with learning difficulties is offered one night a week for both the students and their parents. Toward the end of each meeting, the parents and students meet separately, and they always end with refreshments and informal discussion. One mother said, "It's so helpful to know I'm not the only one going through this. I thought I was the only parent who had a child who wouldn't do schoolwork."

Local businesses sponsor and support school activities as well. The Community Garden is an example. It's funded and guided by local businesses, and students run it. They plant, weed, maintain, and harvest. They keep records. In the summer, they run tours for the community, explaining the organic gardening techniques they use. In the fall, they run a farmers' market and use their income to sustain the program. They usually have enough of a harvest to contribute to a local food bank as well. Other community-sponsored projects include the Environmental Restoration Project, the Butterfly Project (both connected to the science program), and Habitat for Humanity.

There are many other less formal school activities to which parents are invited. In the fall, there is a picnic where parents, teachers, and students meet for hamburgers, hot dogs, some games, and informal discussion. Every October the school holds its RoadRunner, a short cross-country race in which hundreds of students participate. Parents join teachers in shouting and cheering for the runners. Hudson also holds recognition breakfasts for students who have made significant improvements in some aspect of their school lives. Parents are invited, and the student band entertains. These activities serve as ways for parents and teachers to get to know one another, stay in touch, and work together on substantive issues.

Hudson is also responsive to parent problems. The school cafeteria is open 1 hour before school begins so students can have breakfast, work, or simply talk with one another. This was begun to accommodate parents who need to leave for work earlier than the school buses arrive to pick up their children.

The district and school offer evening programs that focus on parent needs, such as ways of supporting study skills, getting to know young adult literature, and dealing with your adolescent. The principal works hard to support the PTA, which plans and offers effective programs for parents as well as students. Hudson also has an extremely active parent–community music group. They practice at the school and hold an annual concert that is very well attended. Parents run clubs (e.g., Olympics of the Mind) and speak at team and school events and in classes, where their special knowledge extends the topics the students are studying.

Typical schools, in comparison, don't connect with parents and the community in these substantive and far-reaching ways. They sometimes make school visits to local businesses and on rare occasion invite a speaker, but not much else. They have a narrower range of offerings and less interaction.

In short:

- Make your school a welcome place for parents, where they can stop by uninvited.
- Partner with local workplaces in ways that extend students' school experiences and draw community members in and make them feel involved.
- Draw on parents' expertise and experience in coursework.
- Use community and civic organizations as a source of knowledge and participation.
- Offer parent–student learning events.

THE SCHOOL AS A COMMUNITY RESOURCE

Schools that work contribute to their communities, a rarity in more typical schools. In addition to the community helping the school, Springfield has become a resource to its community. It applied for a grant that funded its parent center, a gathering place for parents and community members. It offers courses and meetings on a range of subjects from computer skills to literacy, courses to help you help your child, and courses for your own learning. It also provides advice and access to community resources and services. Once a year, a parent summit offers a day of presentations on a variety of topics. Parents are on the advisory board of the parent center, so they're involved in planning and overseeing the quality and effectiveness of its offerings.

Hudson also reaches out beyond the parents, to the community at large. For example, some students spend several weeks teaching senior citizens to use computers and navigate the Internet. This requires them to hone their own computer knowledge and pushes them to learn even more as their aged students asked questions or problems arose. A volunteer coordinator serves as an outreach person who makes connections between community and school needs and arranges for volunteers. Parents work regularly in the library, for instance, and the library offers discussions about children's books for parents. Sometimes the school, and other times the district, sponsors speakers to address issues such as child development or drug-related problems. Parent–community reading groups are ongoing. At Hudson, it's part of the district, school, and team culture to view parents and local residents as essential members of the school community and as vital to student success.

Typical schools have a qualitatively different way of offering to the community. One high school, for instance, has two separate school administrations, one for the day and one for the evening program, with no interaction at all. A teacher said, "We have students who are returning after many years out of school. We have students who have dropped out within the last 10 years coming back for a GED. We have students who are failing day school. We have parents who are taking classes, and also some of our students. But the right hand doesn't know what the left hand is doing." This school also has a full-service health clinic, but it was not being used very much during the 2 years we studied the school.

In short:

- Find ways to enrich the community—in school and out. Make your school a presence.
- Connect students to the community, contributing to it as well as learning from it.

CARING COUNTS, TOO

Schools that work well have a culture of community. They exude caring and go the extra mile to make it happen. The educational program gains strength through behaviors and activities such as shared remembrances, family conferences before problems escalate, exciting programs that show respect for community knowledge and learning, substantive community involvement, and conscientious role modeling, supporting, listening, and following through. But these are far from superficial. The kind of caring they demonstrate grows from their sincere concern for the students' and families' well-being and for fairness, justice, and equity at school and in the world—as well as from the deep belief that by reaching out as teachers and as human beings they can not only help their students learn better but also help create the kind of society in which they can all improve their lot. Springfield is one such school. It's unusual only because it's in a kind of setting where some people say that parental involvement is impossible and unwanted. Yet the activities at Springfield make it clear that, in fact, significant involvement can happen and can make a difference for all concerned. Hudson also exudes caring. Its students are younger, its demographics different, and its offerings not exactly the same as Springfield's. The particular pattern of activities that schools use to engender a helpful, caring, and connected community differs from place to place, but all unusually successful schools that I've studied have created similar degrees of involvement through a variety of programs tailored to their own communities.

Now, rate your school, using the chart on the next page.

How Effective Is Your School?—Parent and Community Involvement

			RATE YOUR SCHOOL	
MORE EFFECTIVE SCHOOLS:	LESS EFFECTIVE SCHOOLS:	Doing Well	Needs Improvement	Needs to Get Started
Invite parents and community members to substantively engage in helping to solve problems and shape the school.	Invite superficial involvement and no engagement in decisions.			
Invite parents to sit on a range of school committees.	Are selective about parent involvement.			
Meet problems by setting up collaborative school–community problem-solving committees.	Keep the community out of the loop when problems arise.			
Involve parents in learning about and participating in all aspects of students' school lives.	Involve parents primarily when their child has a problem.			
Keep parents involved in the curriculum, instruction, and assessment loop.	Keep parents out of curriculum and instruction.			
Call substantive meetings where parents are actively involved in understanding problems and discussing potential solutions.	Call update meetings where parents are told what the changes are.			
Welcome parents at all times.	Frown upon unscheduled visits.			
Go beyond report cards in keeping parents up to date on how their children are doing.	Rely on report cards for updates.			
Work with parents to head off problems.	Don't call parents in until problems become full-blown.			
Form partnerships with local business and civic groups to enhance students' instructional experiences.	Use business and civic sites as places to visit.			
Use parent and community expertise in the classroom to augment instruction.	Keep instruction separate from the community.			
Collaborate with local colleges and universities in a range of educational projects.	Consider such collaborations intrusive.			
Act as a community resource.	Take from the community but don't give to it.			

Good Schools Are Possible Everywhere:
One Neighborhood, Two Schools

UNTIL NOW I've been describing educational features that are demonstrably different in schools that work well and those that don't. In this chapter, I'll try to elaborate on those differences by painting a fuller picture of two schools, one highly successful and one with problems. The important thing to remember as you read about them is that they're in the same neighborhood. Ruby is a middle school and Lincoln,[1] a high school. Brothers and sisters go to both schools. Younger children grow up and study at Ruby, then move on to Lincoln. Their parents get report cards, go to meetings, help their children, and want them to succeed at both schools. Yet how the two schools operate, what's expected of teachers, how they teach, and what students learn couldn't be more different. As you read, look for the features of effective schools that I've discussed in the previous chapters. You'll see differences in overall administration, in the professional lives of the teachers, and in the instruction the students receive.

THE NEIGHBORHOOD

Both schools are in a high-poverty and high-crime area on the outskirts of a large city in Texas. Because there are lots of open fields with pastures and cattle as well as large undeveloped areas, it feels more rural than urban. If you were to drive through the community, you'd see a mix of small houses and poorly maintained multistory garden apartments. Buildings have been abandoned; trash blows from one open area to another and lodges next to buildings. The houses have grates on the windows, as do the cashier areas in the local gas station and food market. A short walk from one of the schools is a take-out restaurant frequented by the teachers and local workers who want a quick (and good) lunch. The order, preparation, and cash register areas are behind a large Plexiglas barrier. It's a rough neighborhood, but, as in others like it, parents want their children to learn, and they visit school and give support when they have reason to do so.

THE SCHOOLS

Ruby and Lincoln aren't far from one another, and the same racial mix of students attend both schools: approximately 80 percent African American, 15 percent Hispanic, and the rest White and Asian. But this is where the similarity stops. Lincoln High School is welcoming. The grounds are well kept, with pleasant shrubs and comfortable benches outside. The large electrified bulletin board outside has continually changing announcements of parent meetings, test preparation, and community affairs. Graffiti is rare, but when it appears the students are asked to wash it off. The school looks and feels tranquil. When the school buses arrive, students talk with one another as they get off, walk into school quietly, and begin their day. The principal greets them at the school door, and the teachers greet them at the classroom doors. Most doors are left open throughout the day, and people come and go naturally. Although the school's iron fence is locked during the day for safety, an inner courtyard is used for work and relaxation.

Ruby, on the other hand, is poorly maintained and disorderly. A high cyclone fence surrounds the school, and trash is evident both inside and outside the fence. The large electrified bulletin board is broken and unused; the few shrubs are not maintained. Students get off the buses in a loud and boisterous fashion, pushing and shouting. A bar on the school door keeps them from entering the building until the appointed time. No one meets them at the school door; when the bar is lifted, they enter in a noisy and jostling mass. When they're in their classrooms, the doors are locked.

This is the outside; let's see the differences once inside. Lincoln's walls are decorated with school photographs, mementos, student artwork, and projects. Parents are always in the front office. The secretaries are friendly toward the parents, as is the principal. Before getting to the reason for the visit, they discuss family and local events. During class time, the principal and assistant principal are often in the corridors and classrooms, with friendly smiles and greetings to all. They stop and talk to students, teachers, support and maintenance staff. The English classrooms are in one wing of the building, so teachers can more easily share ideas and catch each other for informal meetings. The classroom doors are open; when students are at work, teachers sometimes take a minute to talk with one another or to visitors. Inside and outside the classrooms, you hear pleasantly busy conversation. A look into the classroom reveals students who are engaged in their work, whether as a whole class, in a group, or alone. They look and sound involved. Their teachers speak with them in ways that seem instructive, helpful, and directed to their needs. The entire school staff takes responsibility for student behavior. Misbehavior is quickly stopped with a talking-to by whichever adult is closest, sometimes even before a problem starts. When the bell rings, students leave class talking about the work they've just been doing or about things they need to do for the next class. Teachers know their students and remind them quietly when they misbehave. The school's stated core values that everyone follows are safety, student learning, excellence, and civility.

Ruby is quite different. Indoors you see barren walls and flaking paint. The school office is often empty of visitors; photocopied reminders for parents about proper behavior and potential school actions greet the visitor upon entry. Although the secretaries are courteous, no one in the office engages visitors in conversation. The principal keeps to her office, which is relaxed, with easy chairs and stuffed animals. Parents who have an appointment are shown in. The English classes are spread out across the entire building, following no plan. The teachers rarely see each other. During class time, the halls are empty and few sounds are heard from the classrooms. The windows in the doors of most classrooms are covered with paper; you can't see in—or out. There are no visible conversations. The vice principal is in charge of discipline. He uses a megaphone to call for quiet in large areas such as the lunchroom. When students misbehave, they're sent to him. When the bell rings, students leave class in the same boisterous manner they entered, often crumpling their papers and dropping them on the hallway floors or as they leave the building. The principal has set discipline as a priority; she feels good discipline must precede learning.

THE PARENTS AND COMMUNITY

The schools get on with parents differently, too. Lincoln is an anchor in the community; it offers many parent education meetings and courses, helps parents learn to help their children, lends parents books, and supports them in many other ways. Parents recommend courses as well as take them, and they serve on a variety of committees. Administrators and teachers involve parents in discussion about issues that matter and try to be helpful. When a child misses school too often, shows changes in behavior, or is acting-out, parents are quickly called in to discuss the problem and avert trouble before it starts or escalates. Local clergy sometimes participate in parent–teacher discussions. The principal courts local help. Along with local businesses, she arranges lunches for the mayor and police chief and enlists their support for safety as well as ongoing and special projects. The faculty consider community support essential to their well-being and, in the face of growing home-schooling and privatization, want to be a school of choice.

Ruby also holds meetings for parents, although fewer. However, these are generally information-giving sessions. Someone speaks about an issue or tells parents what to do to help their children do better on tests, and then the meeting ends. Greetings and good wishes, individual conversations, opportunities to discuss concerns and help parents think things through are missing. The principal believes in maintaining good relations with parents; when she meets with them, she's warm and friendly and let's them know she cares. Parents are contacted about student behavior, usually after a problem has blossomed or gotten out of hand.

As you can see, although the schools are in the same district and even the same community, they're run very differently. Lincoln also has a long history of being a well-run school, effectively using site-based management and fostering a sense of community. Many of the teachers have worked there for a decade or more, and there is very little teacher turnover. The dean of instruction, who has been at the school for more than 20 years, instituted and has maintained collaborative planning and joint problem solving both within and across departments. High academic achievement is a goal she and the faculty hold to. The present principal, who has been at the school for 10 years, is a good administrator and outreach person, and delegates well. Instruction is not her specialty, so she gives this authority to the dean, who has a strong track record.

Ruby, on the other hand, has a shaky history. When the principal was hired just over 5 years ago, the school was in receivership for a long-time record of low test scores. Although some teachers have been working there for many years, there is also frequent turnover and no history of instructional support. The principal was selected to run this school due to her success elsewhere, but her old procedures don't work at Ruby. She hired a dean of instruction to oversee the instructional program. But the principal has no strong instructional philosophy of her own, didn't involve faculty in hiring the dean, and used test scores but not professional development or instructional approaches as a hiring criteria. The dean of instruction is a hardworking loner, someone who prepares materials for teachers and makes presentations but doesn't work with them in problem-solving sessions. The principal was able to remove teachers she considered ineffective but had no master plan in hiring new teachers, nor did she or the dean of instruction have a plan to help the newly hired teachers be more effective than those who had left.

DIFFERENT RESPONSES TO TESTS

By now, I'm sure you've guessed that the schools' tests scores are very different and that they respond to the present testing movement differently. In reading and writing, Ruby is one of the lowest-performing schools in the district, while Lincoln is quite high. Lincoln's students scored higher in writing than one of the top upper-middle-class schools in the district, one considered to be among the most prestigious. Let's see why.

At Lincoln, the administrators and faculty believe their students can do well on tests and in school, and they take it as their responsibility to make it happen. They meet often to develop ways to help students become involved in and successful at their coursework; offer experiences that will prepare them for life after high school; are responsive to standards, tests, and outside concerns; and look ahead to what else might be needed. While they work hard at developing special school programs and course offerings that engage as well as instruct, they also keep up with district-wide projects. One teacher at each grade level has been asked to work on a district-wide instructional guide committee to align instruction with the state standards and tests and to develop sample lessons for teachers to use. The chair sees to it that the English teachers are all involved in developing the guide; although only some are on the committee, they get updates, review materials, and give feedback to their colleagues during department meetings. The chair and teachers know it's to their and their students' benefit to stay involved and have a hand in the development of the guide. In addition to the work within the department, the dean of instruction meets with representatives of each academic department to discuss students' learning, work on curriculum, and evaluate how these affect test scores and learning. Administrators and faculty know the tests are important for their students; although the school scores are already quite good, they want to help them do even better. Their intent, as always, is to refine the academic program and instructional approaches in ways that will help their students do better at everything.

As a matter of course, teachers and administrators keep an ear to the central office; working on committees and attending meetings help them know and have a hand in shaping what's being considered. When they heard the state test was going to change, the Lincoln chair called meetings to discuss different formats and content that might be included and what they would need to do next. When they found that they had already been using the kinds of editing activities that were being discussed for the next state assessment, they reviewed exactly how they were teaching these. As part of their proactive test prep, their goal was to increase coherence from class to class and across grades. And they shared lessons to be sure they were on the same page in carrying it through.

Ruby is also responsive to tests, but in a different way. Because the principal had been brought in to raise scores, her major assignment for the new dean of instruction was also to raise test scores. She leaves test prep fully up to the dean. The dean studies scores and provides materials for classroom use. She developed a faculty handbook that was given to all English teachers. Each year, she purchases brush-up and practice material and develops her own test-preparation exercises for teachers to use. These are placed in teachers' mailboxes or given out at meetings. Ruby teachers are also on the district-wide instructional guide committee, but, unlike their colleagues at Lincoln, there's no mechanism for them to share what they learn.

Encouraged by the dean of instruction to prepare students for the test, the teachers put their regular curriculum aside and rely on test teaching, review, and practice. Initially, they spent half the year, and now almost the full year, practicing for the state test, primarily using the materials provided by the dean of instruction. When the district supervisor for English language arts sent a working draft of the new test to all administrators and teachers asking for feedback, each teacher received the memo separately and responded separately—or didn't. And test preparation continues in much the same way as before: skills practice in class every day with a focus on grammar and punctuation—also persuasive writing and summary, generalizations, and outside information because "they're on the TAAS [state test]." And every Friday for about 25 minutes of instruction time, everything stops and teachers distribute handouts provided for them with information about the objective they'll be working on. For the next half-hour, a lesson comes over the loudspeaker from the dean of instruction, while teachers in each classroom see to it that their students do the work. "It's test review time," the voice says. "I will give you time to get your materials. We're going to work on specific details."

During our study, students' writing scores at Lincoln went up and at Ruby went down. At Lincoln the usual set of review and planning meetings and discussions began. "Don't say this is for the TAAS," the dean of instruction reminded, "do it for good reading and writing. We have to make the test work for us." At Ruby, the principal said, "You have to get the scores up. You have to study and teach the core knowledge . . . work harder."

DIFFERENT NOTIONS OF PROFESSIONALISM

As you can see, each school in its own way is trying to raise student performance, but there are differences in how they're going about it and in what they believe will make it happen. Lincoln operates as a professional community, always planning, sharing information, and examining itself with an eye to improvement. The dean of instruction, teachers, and chairs work together and are professionally proactive. They believe their knowledge will help them fine-tune instruction and improve student learning. They keep up with the field and with changes in policy, and they actively scrutinize their programs and their teaching in light of student needs and changing demands (such as the state tests and standards). The principal supports professional involvement, and the dean of instruction encourages it. At Ruby, district- and school-sponsored meetings and workshops are called and attended, but additional professional development is left to the individual. Teachers do it on their own, outside of school, or not at all. There are no mechanisms to use these experiences within the school.

New teachers have very different experiences, too. At Lincoln new teachers get a district-sponsored, intensive first-year mentoring experience. The new teachers and their mentors take a course together and both keep journals containing their descriptions and reflections on their lessons, students, teaching materials, workshops, and collaborations. They read each other's journals and discuss them together. In addition, informal mentoring goes on all the time. More experienced teachers share lesson plans, explain goals, and discuss teaching approaches and student needs with their new colleagues and make themselves approachable and available to answer questions and help solve problems. At Ruby, the new teachers also get the district-sponsored intensive mentoring, but the process is adhered to differently. Mentors spend less time meeting with and keeping on top of their new colleagues' teaching activities. The other teachers don't offer help.

DIFFERENT ACADEMIC PROGRAMS

As I'm sure you've surmised, the academic programs students receive are as different as the features I've already mentioned. Lincoln keeps a clear focus on the academic program. The dean of instruction believes this is the cornerstone of their success and so do the teachers. She oversees, knows, and keeps in close touch with each department's program and meets with the chairs to ensure programmatic connections across the school. She invites the teachers to meet within and across grade levels and across subject areas to talk about literacy both within the English program and within the other academic programs as well.

Connections and coordination are always the aim, and the faculty work closely to make the program work well. It has its own constantly developing curriculum (the reworking of the state and district standards and guidelines) that guides all teachers' work and is always under revision based on students' needs. Because the teachers are professionally up to date and also have many opportunities to discuss new ideas and programmatic needs, they've developed a common philosophy about teaching and about English that gives their program consistency and guides them in choosing certain approaches, activities, or materials and not others. Teachers also help choose new teachers—people they feel they can work with who are philosophically compatible but who will add ideas or knowledge and help sharpen the program. And, as I mentioned, they work with the dean of instruction and central office to ensure their program is responsive to changes in the district and state. They constantly explore ways to be sure students have a coherent and related program across all their school literacy experiences. The English teachers work with the reading, ESL, and extra-help teachers to make this happen. They help plan Saturday tutorials and other remedial offerings as well as extracurricular enrichment activities.

In comparison, Ruby teachers receive the state and district standards and guidelines and are expected to use them as their program. The materials that have been developed and ordered provide the bare bones of common experience, but there's no flesh on these bones. Teachers adhere to these individually; beyond the materials, there is little to ensure programmatic consistency. New teachers are hired by the principal and expected to fit in. Except for some friendships among individual teachers, there is little interaction across departments.

Because of its low scores, Ruby has a lot of extra help: tutors, an external reading consultant, and some elementary teacher trainers. Like the other teachers, these specialists are hired by the principal, given their assignments, and expected to provide the instruction the students need. They are not expected to work closely with one another or with the classroom teachers.

Occasional grade-level and department meetings sometimes focus on issues of great concern. For example, at one meeting that took 15 to 20 minutes, the teachers were told to look at the most recent test results, see where their students had done poorly, and adjust instruction as needed. There seemed a bit of confusion about exactly what to do. Neither the chair nor the teachers were certain what was wanted, and no discussion time had been scheduled. The dean of instruction, who had analyzed the scores and planned the assignment, was not present at the meeting or at the next department meeting 2 months later. That next meeting was called by the department chair and lasted more than 40 minutes (one class period), with a full agenda. It began with a discussion of books, followed by a review by the chair of benchmark items. Then the teachers were given a handout with students' names grouped according to items they had missed on the test. The teachers were told to analyze their students' results in relation to the benchmark items and to tailor instruction. There were a few comments but no focused discussion or move for a joint plan of action. Following this, the chair told the teachers that the principal had hired teachers from another school to remove the neediest students from their classrooms and tutor them. There was no organizational strategy in place to hear the teachers' opinions or questions or to get beyond the "fix-up" attempts to more systematic program building.

DIFFERENT KINDS OF INSTRUCTION

Now let's look inside the classroom, at instruction. Lincoln students are busy, always involved. Sometimes they have whole-class meetings, sometimes they work alone, sometimes they work on things in pairs or larger groups, sometimes they go to the library, sometimes they sit at computers. There are few blank stares. They're involved in thoughtful and minds-on learning. At Ruby, students work primarily in whole-class groups with the teacher up front and do seatwork alone. When they do work together, their primary concern is to figure out what the teacher is after—to get the right answer.

At Lincoln, even the lowest-performing students are taught to think, discuss, and write about new ideas in ways that clarify their understandings and make them better learners. As a matter of course, everyone is expected to have ideas and participate in discussions and classwork. Class-time is active because students are taught not merely to read and write and understand their literature but also to think about the content in highly literate ways. For example, Vanessa Justice tried to help her students look across texts at pervasive themes in literature and life and also to be able to do this across genres. Her tenth-grade students did research in the library and wrote reports about the Harlem Renaissance. She used this to lead into their reading of *Their Eyes Were Watching God*, by Zora Neale Hurston, and then used the novel to move into poetry from the same era. She then connected these works to others written at other times. Discussion, projects, writing, and role play were all used to help the students understand not only the works and the writers' crafts but also the literary tradition they represented, how it affected both the writers and their audience, and how it differed from other literary traditions.

At Lincoln, when students need help they get it, but the expectations for thoughtful work don't change. Sometimes the teachers help by asking guiding questions, suggesting think-abouts or providing models. When veteran teacher Viola Collins wanted to help her students think in more complex ways about the literature they were reading, she modeled the thinking for them, thinking aloud or showing them her written ideas. She'd do this on the first portion of the text and discuss it with the class. And if it was needed, she'd keep it going with her modeling and their discussion throughout the novel. Her goal was for the students to try out new ways for thinking on their own She also helped her students improve as writers. Teaching writing and grammar came with the writing of sentences, using whatever vocabulary they were doing at the time, as well as in more extended writing. Students wrote 5 or 10 sentences, which she would carefully edit and return. These assignments became individual grammar and diction lessons for each student, as the patterns of errors began to show. The longer writing assignments were completed in workshop settings with anyone free to ask questions and discuss ideas. She also had individual meetings with students during these times, to offer specific help. These workshop classes were also times when grammar needs were addressed. When it became clear there was an issue several students were having trouble with, she would bring them together for a minilesson.

Lincoln teachers focus on skills and want their students to understand why they're important. They think it's critical for their students to understand the social and grammatical conventions that underlie why we say things this way and not that—so they'll be able to make language decisions on their own, in new situations. Students learn to look for the underlying logic behind language choice and usage. They see language in context, are asked to identify what works well or is wrong, correct it, and explain why. They become "analysts." They discuss language use and the circumstances in which one choice works better than another. Instruction at Lincoln teaches students the kinds of literacy skills and knowledge needed to make them stronger readers and writers, but always in the context of using it for some purpose.

At Ruby, skills are taught by rules and practice. For example, sixth-grade teacher Shaney Young asked her students to open their books and then read as they followed along, "Verbs tell what the subject of a sentence does or is. The verb is the most important word in the predicate. Two types of verbs are action and being verbs. Number one, Mr. Martinez coaches our team. What kind of verb is that?" As a class, they complete assignments such as this one, check answers, and review the rules. Reading instruction follows the text or texts the teachers are using, as well as the reading test preparation activities that have been prepared. The pattern of Young's activity looks much like her grammar lesson: set questions about the reading passages, with set answers that students must give. Ruby's main goal is for the test scores to improve, and there is the belief that the chosen materials will accomplish this. The teachers say they would like to do more but feel there isn't time. To do more would be "off the task of efficient teaching and learning."

THE TWO SCHOOLS: A RE-VIEW

What a difference between the schools, you think. Yet both are hardworking. It's their beliefs about what works best and how it can best be carried through that differ so radically. Lincoln's principal is a good administrator. She came to an already successful school and delegated authority to people she trusted. She oversees the school in ways that maintain the philosophy and programs but leave room for change. Viola Collins calls her "an instructional empowerer, a woman who likes others with ideas and energy. If you can communicate your ideas to her and how they fit into the program of instruction, she'll help you. If she sees some opportunity for the school, she'll try to funnel someone's interest to it." She maintains good relations with the faculty and community, hosts parties for celebrations, and "keeps the door open." In comparison, Ruby operates more rigidly. It's held together by a fairly tight system of unwritten rules and precedents that define what's possible and how things should be done. It's a polite school, with an ethos of not talking about one another. (In a subtle way, this cuts off helping one another.) The principal says administrators and staff are "family." She holds gatherings such as pot lucks and parties for the faculty and staff, but they don't talk about work. The individuals who were chosen to turn the school around haven't been able to do so, although they've tried. The features of successful schools that I discussed in Chapters 2 through 6 are all missing.

CHAPTER 8

The Road to Change

CLEARLY, THERE'S A HUGE difference between schools that work well and those that don't. And in the differences we can see where change is possible. If nothing else, I hope the previous chapters have provided a vision of what schools that work well look like, how they operate, and what they do to make a difference. They respond to the current testing movement but go much further: They create professional climates for teachers to learn and do their work, develop challenging academic programs, continually improve instruction, and interact productively with parents and community. They're goal oriented but open, organized but inclusive, coherent but flexible, rigorous but humane. And they're within reach.

This chapter has two parts. First I will pull together some of what we've learned from this investigation, and then I will suggest some things you can do to improve schools. Although my study focused primarily on

English and literacy, the organization of the coursework in some schools enabled us to look beyond, to the larger educational environment. It is important, however, to use the discussion and suggestions that follow as a guide, to stimulate inspection and discussion in the context of your own particular situations, disciplines, and realities.

In spite of concerns about national security and the economy, Americans continue to rate education among their top priorities. In Oregon, for example, 4,600 taxpayers who received tax refunds voluntarily donated almost $700,000 of that money to a newly created fund to support public schools,[1] and that sentiment, if not the action, exists nationwide. The time is right for people who care about education to come together, investigate the issues, debate solutions, and act. In some places big changes are needed, and everyone will have to play a part.

The features of successful schools I've described in this book seem, at first glance, to be sensible examples of good administration and good practice. They involve good teaching in well-orchestrated environments with professionals at the helm. But these aren't the practices in most schools across the United States. Excellent schools, those that work well, look and feel different from typical schools; they're marked by an overriding sense of knowledge, organization, and caring. Administrators and teachers work closely with their communities to decide what's needed, work toward common goals, and get ongoing feedback and help. Teachers and administrators are part of a professional community that works together, keeps in touch with new ideas, grows professionally, and creates programmatic coherence and a positive school climate. Parents are involved in an essential sense; their participation helps the school understand the community's perceptions and goals while the school gains community support in meeting challenges and instituting change. Teachers and parents feel that they know what's going on and that they can help shape what happens at school.

More effective schools develop and maintain coherent academic programs and organize instruction in a way that offers students compounded, connected, and thought-provoking experiences across time and across classes. Although teachers are part of an important professional community that gives them knowledge and feedback, there is a larger community—including parents and the local residential and business communities—that has a central role in the school's success. They work together.

Every day, year in and out, there's the belief that all students can learn and that the professional staff must find ways to make it happen. Teachers and parents are empowered to identify problems, explore options, find assistance when needed, and work with others to develop and carry out reform efforts. Besides that, effective schools are comfortable and humane places where parents and community members can talk about students' needs, the public agenda, the school's response to these needs, and the roles that everyone can play. Plans of action are developed on the basis of the particulars of the local community as well as in response to state and national goals. Everyone is on the same page.

In all, from the moment you step inside, the more effective schools are welcoming, collaborative, and professional. A walk through the halls usually shows pride of learning and a sense of continuity; photographs of school events, student artwork, writing, science projects, local prizes and memorabilia, and successes of graduates cover the walls. Students have many opportunities to think about what they enjoy doing and what they do well. They have room to develop a sense of who they might become and what they might do when they finish school.

Classrooms are environments for learning new things and for thinking about those ideas, discussing them, and doing things with them. Students expect and are expected to take new ideas, try them on, work with them, relate them to other things they know, and make them their own. They expect to think and expect to learn; they are almost always minds-on. That's a major difference between the schools that work well and those that don't. The students in the more effective schools engage in interesting activities and think about school content most of the time. That's different from simply sitting quietly, doing what the teacher asks, and even answering all the questions right. The amount of quality, minds-on time differs, as does the depth of thinking. Students have the opportunity to grapple with the ideas they're studying—together, alone, via e-mail, in the library—and reach a deeper and more connected understanding of the new ideas. The students see school as interesting and immerse themselves in the work.

But just as the students are learning, so, too, are the teachers. They keep up with their profession, and they focus on their program, their instruction, and students' responses to it. They know their students and even during lessons keep a third eye on how individual students are responding and what else is needed.

They expect differences among students and treat diversity as an opportune teaching tool. Effective schools are good for everyone; teachers and administrators believe that if they do their jobs well, all students will learn. If this doesn't happen, they look to themselves and what else they can do. They also believe that having students from a variety of home backgrounds in their classes is an intellectually interesting educational opportunity and use it as a way to enrich learning. The way a class is run and the way students are taught to work with one another make a difference. Students are given chances to hear other perspectives and to learn to listen for, question, challenge, analyze, and weigh other points of view and other ways of doing things—as well as to explain, elaborate, defend, analyze, weigh, and rethink their own ideas, interpretations, and ways of doing things.

Teachers use diversity as a way to provoke language use, sharp reasoning, and intercultural as well as content understanding. Homogeneity is seen as less interesting, as setting limits to what students will discuss and think about, either making it more necessary for teachers to bring in other perspectives from the outside or making classes not only less interesting but also intellectually narrow. Teachers try to help their students see diversity in their backgrounds, interests, and histories even in classes where the students are seemingly similar. They help their students look beyond as well as within the class and beyond as well as within their cultures and times to explore possibilities and reach deeper understandings. These teachers go much beyond notions of multicultural literature or writing stories from home and collecting them into a book. They help students ask hard questions that will complicate and enrich their knowledge about the topics at hand.

Teachers in successful schools keep up with research on teaching as well as their subject matter and continually refine their pedagogical know-how—how to teach as well as what. The Association for Supervision and Curriculum Development is concerned that helping teachers gain "the knowledge and tools for successful classroom management and the use of innovative methods to engage students and bolster learning" will get overlooked in the reaction to testing.[2] While this seems to be so in more typical schools, we've seen that academic programs and effective instruction are at the heart of what effective schools worry about and work to refine. They're the topics of study when teachers come together to study, learn, and grow.

And, of course, parent and community involvement are critical in making it all work for students. Parents and students who don't have ties to their schools feel misunderstood by teachers and teachers feel misunderstood by parents.[3] There's a link between parent involvement and academic achievement for all children.[4] Without a doubt, schools need to involve everyone. It makes a difference, and there's too much to lose.

Looking across the chapters, I hope you can see that educators in more typical schools do want their students to do better and usually undertake a variety of efforts to help them improve. But these schools just don't have the organized, highly informed, and participatory features that pervade the more effective programs. Sometimes one or some of the features I've discussed may be in place, but that is not enough. Only when all the features I've discussed come together do they create the climate and add the comprehensiveness needed to excel.

WHAT TEACHERS CAN DO

Teachers' major efforts need to be in planning, monitoring, and carrying out effective academic programs and challenging instruction. This is done most effectively within the department, team, or academy, as well as the classroom. But it can be difficult in a school where collaboration and teacher involvement beyond the classroom have no place. In effective schools, teachers get around this hurdle by using what educational researcher Pam Grossman[5] calls channels—by finding a support path somewhere else. Sometimes there's a dean of instruction who can help arrange meeting time and other support and ensure the work will be used and honed, not ignored. Sometimes there's a districtwide English language arts coordinator or a district director of curriculum and instruction who can involve the faculty in the kinds of collaborative working groups they're looking for and their students need. Preferable to both of these, of course, is approaching the principal with a well-developed proposal. This should include the scope of work (program planning and revision, review and inquiry into instructional methods), the resources needed (time to meet, funds for review materials and school visits or speakers), the intended product (program description, curriculum guide, instructional activities), and the intended time frame. Ideally, an administrator would be assigned to work along with the teachers as a colleague, to help arrange institutional support, and to help see the work is carried through to action.

Test preparation is needed, but the kind I've already discussed, where teachers meet with their colleagues, analyze the test, and reach a deeper understanding of the skills, strategies, and knowledge needed to do well not only on the test but also in school, work, and life. The goals of testing and the preparation for tests need to go beyond the tests themselves. Together, teachers need to review existing curricula and instructional guidelines (or develop them if they don't exist) to ensure that the identified skills and knowledge are incorporated into the ongoing English program. Then effective teaching is needed. It's the infusion of the needed skills and knowledge into the daily life of the classroom and making students aware of how these connect with other things they've learned, will learn, and might use that make a difference.

Remember, the high-stakes tests students must take are a reflection of the education they've had across their school lives, not just what they've done during the current year. No one teacher can ever prepare them enough. Preparing them requires teachers to work together to offer the best and most coherent academic program possible, across the grades. It needs to offer opportunities for an array of literacy skills and knowledge to be taught and used over time, in a variety of activities. Teaching merely the particular kinds of reading and writing genres, strategies, activities, or formats that are called for on the present test will do students a disservice, both for other tests they may have to take and in their ability to meet other literacy demands in school and in life. It's important to avoid getting caught in a drill-for-the-test syndrome, teaching to the test all year. Teachers do better and students will be more successful if they have a rich and varied curriculum that includes but isn't dominated by the literacy activities the test calls for. Instead, teachers need to help students understand the conventional formats that underlie reading and writing (e.g., what to expect in a persuasive or informative piece, or in a mystery or folktale) and how they shape the structure and language used. And, if extra help is needed, they can try to see that the student gets it in class as well as out.

And, of course, teachers need to meet and converse with their colleagues about what they're doing so that they can weave a web of connections across students' school experiences, letting students see and know where the pieces fit—how skills and knowledge are useful in a range of situations. The most successful teachers never forget that effective learning engages students in substantive discussion of challenging content around big ideas. Their classrooms are thoughtful and interactive, giving students time and opportunity to try out new ideas and think things through. In-depth learning doesn't happen without questioning, false starts, pondering, and cogitation. Students' understandings and capacities grow and deepen through substantive conversations with others, and therefore teachers need to plan time for collaborative group discussion, debate, and learning. But to participate in such activities, students need to learn the kinds of questions to ask and the ways to think and talk about new ideas and experiences. So, in addition to the content, teachers need to be sure to teach strategies that guide students in ways to think about and do the work. All this is a tall order, particularly in places where the textbook alone is being used as a guide. Although some of these offer pedagogical advice, they don't replace the need for professional teachers who keep up with their field.

Teachers also need to know their students and understand them as learners, rather than making quick judgments about what they can and can't do. They need to help each student find a way into the material and have the room to mull about the ideas and think things through. This involves maintaining an educational climate that draws students in and involves them in ideas—minds-on. Activities of this sort might involve group projects, debates, or reenactments. All require data gathering, discussion, and thinking things through. And all provide teachers with the opportunity to use different instructional approaches, where needed.[6]

Teachers also need to maintain close working relations with parents as well as the community. Each sees the student in a different context, and the two views aren't always the same. Both need to describe the child's strengths and problems as they see them—be they about behavior, difficulties with particular content, or the boredom of the advanced student—and to find ways to bring the strengths in one setting into the other, while planning extra learning opportunities where needed. Report cards and a parent night once a semester aren't enough for many students. An occasional letter home describing the work they're doing and what they need to do at home is more than greatly appreciated; it helps create the home–school bond that supports learning. Getting together with other teachers to offer a parent workshop, familiarizing them with course content or test expectations, is also useful. It's important to know the parents and caretakers, hear their concerns, and work together.

WHAT SCHOOL ADMINISTRATORS CAN DO

First, administrators need to create a professional community of adult problem solvers and learners within their school. Effective schools are always in a cycle of self-study, professional inquiry, planning, experimentation, and reflection—about their organizational performance as well as their student performance. The two go hand in hand. All stakeholders need to be involved. And that's what school administrators need to put into place. The goal isn't merely to earn high test scores (this will be only one outcome) but to develop interesting, interested, and capable students who attend a school that has its own mark, its own culture, its own way of doing things that grows from where it is and who its students are and shapes the kinds of changes that are made and what's even considered as desirable. Kent Peterson,[7] education professor at the University of Wisconsin, talks about positive and toxic school cultures. On the one hand, you have a school community with a shared way of thinking and talking about values and goals, stories of success, collaboration, and learning; on the other hand, you have a school that lacks a clear sense of purpose and ways to talk and has a climate that discourages collaboration. A positive school culture is the critical first step administrators need to foster and is the outgrowth of much collaborative inquiry, extensive discussion, and the development of common values.

Professional growth goes hand in hand with a positive school culture. Joellen Killion,[8] an educator with the National Staff Development Council, lists several features of schools that excel in professional development. They're not too different from some my study points out: opportunities for teacher learning, including resources, time, and systemic support; clear and focused goals; recognition for success; time to make it happen; shared governance; rewards; and funding where needed. Successful schools develop a distinction, a mark that identifies them. You know what they stand for and what they offer students. Some may be more traditional and others more progressive; some may offer almost all instruction within the school and others integrate it within community settings; some may form alliances and networks with other schools while others might collaborate with a local university as a research and development site; some might apply for school reform funds from such sources as the Annenberg or Pew Foundations. But these alone aren't the mark of distinction any more than the teaching materials are a mark; it's the philosophy about schooling, why the school chose one or another and how it carries the philosophy through in everything it does, that makes the mark.

If it's successful, the mark of distinction is very important. It's what creates coherence in the academic program and in approaches to instruction, provides a way of avoiding fads, and creates an expectation that everyone can rely on to understand what is expected and how things get done. In this era of increasing school choice, the distinction is important. It helps in selecting teachers, being understood within the field, and responding to problems. It also gives parents a way to select a school for their children. Some want more traditional schools while others want more progressive ones. Some may seek cultural and academic enrichment while others want connections to the world of work. Some students may do better in more open environments and some with more structure. All may be effective schools, but the mark of distinction lets each be consistent and understood.

The result of all this would be different, not similar, schools. Of course all would be aiming for the most effective education for all their students. Whatever their mark, they need to aim at least to meet national and state standards, if not surpass them; students will need not only to do well at school but also to pass the tests and meet other externally set requirements.

In addition to developing the school culture, administrators need to reach out to the larger community in ways I've already described. Communities need to be regarded as co-constructors of the school environment and the school's success. The principal can't go it alone, no matter how large a faculty and support staff is at hand. Teams and committees and voices in governance are needed. Teachers, parents, and community members all need to be involved, all the time. Teamwork pays off. It's that essential attitude that needs to underlie governance.

Hand in hand with governance is the opening of school doors to the community. In addition to offering after-school clubs and courses for students, schools should also draw in the community by creating courses for adults, be they about books, child development, computers, community affairs, or gardening (or anything that's right for your locality). Sometimes parents and children will have a chance to go to school together, helping them feel a mutual connection to the school. This becomes a good base for supporting both school needs and student achievement.

WHAT PARENTS CAN DO

I've described the what teachers and administrators can do, but what about parents? Many parents feel powerless, with little for them to personally do to help improve their school. But their children's education is at stake and they can't wait to be invited. A collaborative community is a critical element that's present in effective schools, and if it's not there, someone needs to get it started. If no one else is doing it, parents can try to form a committee of interested community members, administrators, and teachers to get the conversation going. Representation of all groups is critical. It's got to be open and transparent so no one will feel something is being done without their knowledge; it requires true collaboration. Voices need to be heard, but the goal will be to turn what might have been negative complaint sessions into productive explorations of possibilities: committees set up, speakers invited, visits to effective schools planned, self study undertaken—all followed by oral reports and open discussion. If needed, a moderator from a civic group or the school of education at a local university may be helpful in moving the collaboration along. As most of us know, it's difficult to get people to talk to one another when they're not used to it—or to trust each other, set a common goal, and work together to reach it. It will take time and someone who's willing to keep the process going. Keep focused. Keep everyone informed. Develop a communication network, send out newsletters, hold regular events, arrange discussion meetings around predetermined topics—work towards a stated and common goal.

Another step parents can take is to find ways to involve local businesses and community members in students' learning experiences. Every community has people with special hobbies, interests and talents, and life experiences. There are also specialized businesses or corporations that can substantively enrich students' learning experiences, while at the same time fostering ties to the community. Luis Moll,[9] an educational researcher, calls them funds of knowledge. Bringing local funds of knowledge out of the community and into the school validates what parents as well as schools know, elaborates the content students learn, and can bridge the home–school gap for students—and for parents. Of course, as we've seen, businesses and corporations can also become excellent partners in course offerings, special programs, and planned internships targeted to overlaps between school curricular content and community strengths. To get this going, start a Business Advisory Council. One of their first tasks could be to develop a Community Speakers and Talent Bureau. On the list would be every willing person with skills or knowledge who can augment the curriculum, from accountants to mechanics to zoo employees. Instead of planning trips where students simply see people on the job, work with teachers to develop hands-on experiences that get the students involved in using the ideas they've been learning at school within the work-world environment. Perhaps they can even prepare something that will be useful to that workplace. Make it a course–community collaboration.

Using the schools I've described in this book as a model, it becomes obvious that no one group—be it teachers, administrators or parents—can go it alone and institute the substantive and pervasive features that make schools work well. The steps that need to be taken on the road to change involve all three working together—listening, studying, creating, and reflecting as a multifaceted community of educational change agents, stronger and more responsive for the partnership.

WHAT NEXT?

Even as people continue to want more effective schools and increased learning, the reaction to the high-stakes testing movement is splintering. Not only have the concerns and demonstrations I discussed in Chapter 1 continued, but newspapers are beginning to report increases in school dropout rates.[10] Whether these are true figures or not needs further investigation, but the fears of increased school dropouts in reaction to high-stakes tests and their impact on students have begun to be a concern. Changes must be made to improve student learning, without turning off a generation of students. Parents and the community need to feel schools are educating young people well; teachers and administrators need to feel they're successful professionals who can and do make it happen; and students need to feel they can make it.

While tests can be a good way for districts and states to monitor the overall performance of large groups of students in an overall and general measure of school effectiveness over time, we need to be careful about using any one test as an indicator of student success. To know how well students are doing, we need to consider how well they're doing at what: in their classwork on a day-to-day basis, in their class tests, on tests that ask them to discuss information they know and to approach a new problem using what they already know or are just coming to know. Each gives us a different and important window on student learning.

All of us know that there are people who take tests well and those for whom tests are a disaster. I have a computer programmer friend who is so test-phobic that after moving to a new state, she had to take the drivers' written test three times before passing it. But I had helped her practice and knew she knew what was in the manual as well as anyone else. She persevered and got through, but her score never was indicative of what she actually knew. For schoolchildren one test doesn't tell enough, and several tries before you're out doesn't make sense when we want all students to succeed. We need multiple measures—not just state exams, but a variety of local and classroom measures—in order to understand what students know and to help us make decisions about the multiple kinds of help that can be mobilized when needed. The structure and consequences for students need to come from a broader-based data set. Don't lower standards; don't change expectations. But include a number of measures to be determined and managed closer to home. It's part of the collaborative and professional ethos that works so well in the more effective schools and that needs to be put into place more widely. Every school community needs to work together to create not only a caring environment but one that's taking everything into account and is aimed at being wonderful at what it does: educating children well. Nothing less will do.

Further, large-scale testing instruments are useful for tracking progress and comparing performance across schools and regions but limited in what they can tell us about what students can or cannot do. This is where the up-to-date and highly professional teaching staff comes in. With many opportunities to see students respond to new material, to work and solve problems in a variety of activities, teachers can work together to understand not only where students are but also what they need and what works best for them at a particular point in time—to be the responsive teachers every student deserves.

But there's a caveat. At this point in American history, high-stakes tests (with their consequences for students) have become part of our national and state culture, and to get, keep, or change jobs, today's high school graduates will need to have passed these hurdles—to show they can do what society at this time says is important and has decided they must do. Remember, in Chapter 2 I said that standards and tests change as societal conditions, goals, and politics change. Although we can expect change (whether in the long or short run—we never know until it's happened), whatever standards and tests are in place at a particular point in time are an integral part of the environment that will play a significant role in determining a child's future. So, while some of us may not agree with the testing movement and may even be helping the backlash rumble grow into a roar, at the same time we can't forget the youngsters whose school years are now. They must get through them well; they have too much too lose. And, as you've seen from the examples I've given, the characteristics of excellent schools, those that work well, are qualities that should ensure excellent educational programs for all students, for all time.

In reading this book, I hope you see that I've tried to offer some new concepts that can make real changes in how schools conceive of and organize for learning, and how teachers, administrators, parents, and communities can work together to make a difference. Above all, I hope these changes can help nurture the kinds of students who can read, write, and use language effectively and who can think flexibly and deeply. Of course I want them to pass the high-stakes tests (it's important to them in our society, at this time), but I want so much more than that. I also want them to have choices—to be able to gain knowledge and learn new skills and understandings over time and to explore possibilities and ponder options as they shape and reshape their own lives and the world around them. Schools that work well can make this happen.

☆ CHAPTER 9 ☆

Frequently Asked Questions

THE ISSUES I HAVE BEEN dealing with in the previous eight chapters are ones that educators deal with throughout their professional lives; the issues and arguments are familiar questions of school organization and management, curriculum, instruction, and assessment. Parents, on the other hand, approach educational problems from the very personal perspective of their own children's experiences. They ask their questions in different but no less important ways. Thus this closing chapter reformulates the issues addressed earlier, and adds a few new ones, in response to the questions that parents ask.

I spend a good deal of time traveling across the United States, making presentations and having discussions about my research. Often parents are in the groups. When they are, certain questions keep coming up. Some of my responses follow. They fall into four categories: those involving decisions or actions parents and caretakers need to make at home, strategies for connecting with school, information about why schools do or don't teach certain things, and special needs. I'll take them one category at a time.

HOME DECISIONS

Question #1: Nowadays parents and caretakers have more choice about where to send their children, in both public and private schools. How do I decide? What should I look for?

Answer: As I said in Chapter 8, schools are different—and should be. Before you choose, you need to know how they're different and how those differences affect the environment your child will become part of, as well as what and how your child will experience each day. Schools have different philosophies about school structure, teaching and learning, and the most important quality they want students to leave their school with. Some are student centered or progressive; some are more traditional. Some value socialization and human understanding and others put their highest focus on academics. Some stress discipline and keep tight rules; others want students to learn to monitor themselves. That's good for you to know; you've got to choose the one that's best for you and your child. Almost every school has a mission statement and description of its policies, goals, and programs available at the school office. Get a copy and read it. Know your child, know what's important to you, and use this knowledge as a yardstick when you check the school out.

1. Start by thinking about your child as a learner, at home and with friends. List some traits. Some children respond better to a more structured environment, some to a less structured one. Some don't know where to start and rarely follow things through unless they have someone working along with them or unless they have short goals and checkpoints set for them where they can stop and get feedback. Other children need to be left alone to work things out for themselves once a task is given. They need guidance, too, but in response to what they're doing rather than as a way to get started. Some children need to move and talk as they work and learn; others are distracted by this. Most are in the middle. But if your child is in either of the first two groups, try to find a school that matches.
2. Also, think about the aspects of your child's upbringing that matter a great deal to you. Some parents consider disciplined behavior and cour-

tesy very important and want to reinforce this to their children. To them, adult guidance, monitoring, and enforcement are very important. Others feel strongly that their children need to have a minimum of adult intervention and to learn to make decisions on their own. For them, adult notions of courtesy and decorum will develop over time and shouldn't get in the way of self-expression and more childlike behaviors. The first group of parents are bothered by a school where students seem unruly; the second group are bothered if the students are too compliant. Most parents are in the middle. But if you're in either the first or second group, sending your child to a school that's contrary to what matters to you and your family will only create tensions. You will be uncomfortable not only when you visit school but also when your child's friends visit your home and when your own children begin to act like they do at school. Learn what the school expects, how these expectations are carried out, and then decide if this feels comfortable for you and your family.

3. You'll also want to know some general information about the school: its academic record, average class size, percent of students going on to college (and where they go), kinds of parent involvement, extra enrichment offerings, and the backgrounds of the students. Almost all schools make a lot of information available on the Internet as well as in printed materials you can get from the school and main office.

4. Beyond this background information, it's also important to visit a school if you can. Stand outside as children enter and leave. Does what you see feel comfortable to you? Can you imagine your child among the others? Step inside, and on the way to the office, look at the walls, hallways, rooms you pass. Do they feel comfortable to you? Can you imagine your child there? Then make an appointment to visit classrooms. When you get there, look for the kinds of things I've described throughout this book. Here are some ideas:

Take in the environment. Are you comfortable with the way people you see interact with one another? Are you comfortable with how you're treated? What about how the students interact with one another both during and between classes, and even at lunch and play? How are they treated by adults in the school? Look for open doors that welcome parents, teachers, and administrators—a community of learning.

Look into the classrooms. Do you see students who are "minds-on" (cognitively engaged)? Do you see many bored or disengaged students, or a stifled atmosphere? Are there closed doors and covered windows? Get a sense of the classrooms. Try to see a variety of classrooms so your reactions aren't based on a single lesson—even in the best classrooms, some lessons go much better than others. Get the feel and the mood and the way teachers and students interact.

Listen to the learning. Is there a healthy amount of noise as opposed to a series of classrooms completely silent, one after the other? Students need time to ask questions and discuss what they're learning. Listen for enthusiastic interactions around subject matter, not classes out of control.

Look at the layout. What is it like? Are the tables and chairs set up in a variety of ways? Where do teachers stand and students sit? In schools that work well, teachers usually move students and furniture around at times, based on the type of lesson (e.g., circles or squares for discussion, tables for group work, open spaces for drama).

Watch for the activities. Does the school offer opportunities for students to develop broader understandings and interests through special activities? Is there enrichment? Are there clubs? Are there special-interest offerings? Look for schools that value history and culture, that build on the strengths students bring with them, and that encourage development of wider interests.

See the work. Does the school have high expectations? In schools that work well, students are encouraged and stimulated in an inviting and empowering environment. Look for a place that's both supportive and academically challenging.

Check the attitude. Does there seem to be a consistent philosophy underlying the school's goals, curricula, and instruction, or does the school try to be all things to all people? Are teachers and administrators interested in innovation or set in their ways? Are they open to suggestion or defensive? How do they address concerns or handle problems?

Ask about parents. How are parents involved? Does the school encourage parent involvement beyond school trips and cookie sales? If substantive involvement matters to you, ask about committees parents can be on and the kinds of things they do. Speak to parents—ask for names if you don't know anyone.

These are important things to ask about that don't have pat answers. As you think about them, they will help clarify what really matters to you and what's good for your child. If you ask them of teachers, administrators, and parents and use your own antennae when you visit, chances are you'll make a good guess as to whether a school might be a good match for your child.

Question #2: How can I get my child to talk about school? He won't even tell me what he has to do for homework. How can I help him?

Answer: Sometimes we forget that schooltime is your child's time away from home; his private world. Being grilled about it can feel like an invasion of privacy to children. Here are some things to think about and do. First, does everyone at home talk about what they did during the day? Do you? If your family, including the adults, doesn't have a history of sharing what they've done during the day—as a normal way of staying connected—then your child will feel singled out. One way for you to change that is to have a tea-and-talk time in the late afternoon, before dinner, at breakfast, or at any other time when you are together. Serve sodas and a snack everyone will like and start by telling about your day. Let people ask questions and comment; give the speaker support, consolation, helpful feedback. Ask others to take their turns. Next day, tell the next part of your story. It will start slowly, but once away-from-home stories become a ritual, people will keep up with one another and expect the next installment. Don't use this as a time to lecture, just to learn and support. But use what you have learned at another time when you ask about homework. If your child has mentioned studying photosynthesis, for example, you can use it as a lead-in. Instead of asking, "Did you do your homework yet?" or "What do you have to do for homework?" say, "I remember studying about photosynthesis when I went to school, but I don't remember much. I do remember it had to do with plants and sunlight and the color green [whatever you honestly do remember]. Remind me about it, I want to jog my memory." If your child doesn't remember either, you can both look it up and discuss it. Discussing interesting things in your lives and interesting topics you're both (or all) learning can foster a sharing relationship. It lays the groundwork for talk about school and help with it.

If you've tried this and are getting nowhere, you can always contact your child's teacher and set a meeting for the three of you. Then, with your child's knowledge, set up a system for receiving copies of homework assignments or the work that the class is doing. Many teachers use e-mail and might be willing to send copies to interested parents. If not, you, the teacher, and your child might arrange for you to sign each homework assignment when completed. This will give you a chance to discuss it with your child and even work on it together. As you can see, it's developing communicative and collaborative routines with your child that might change things, while nagging or complaining won't.

Question #3: How do I get my child, even my capable one, to connect with school and do the work? She seems more interested in friends and social things, and I'm getting worried.

Answer: First, help her find something to connect with at school and nurture it. What does your child like to do or want do that she can do at school? Might she be interested in playing a musical instrument? Dancing? Acting? Playing a sport? Computers? Doing experiments? Writing? Almost all schools have a variety of activities, one of which might interest your child. Speak with the guidance counselor and arrange for your child to get started. This can also be a way to help your child meet other students, some of whom may be more interested in school than her present friends. It's a way of getting "social things" going at school, where they're intermixed with learning. Having the right friends matters a lot; they can influence how she regards herself as a learner as well as how she spends her time.

If school activities don't work, think of other ways you can expand your child's set of friends to include those who are more interested in school and learning. For example, community and religious groups often offer interesting clubs, study groups, and other opportunities to turn your child on to learning.

Taking a trip with your child can help, too. Speak with the teacher about it first. Enlist her aid. Ask her to tell you what the class will soon be learning. Go someplace interesting (museum, historic site, library, etc.) that is related to what your child will be studying. Have a good time. On your trip, don't talk about class at all, just about what interests you both. Help your child know something about the new topic before it is introduced in class. Then, when the topic is introduced, the teacher can give your child a chance to tell what she did and knows—and to feel good about the topic and herself as a learner.

Question #4: How should I correct my child's grammar and spelling?

Answer: I talked about this a bit in Chapter 5, when the topic was instruction. One thing that doesn't work is correcting your child as he speaks or writes and then telling him to say or write it again. It's a turn-off and often causes a child to use safer and easier language that is more likely to be right. And that inhibits language learning. Instead, you want to expose your child to a language-rich environment, using books, movies, television, technology, and yourself as interesting models of language use. Read with your child and discuss what you are reading (the language and style as well as the content), whatever his age.

This isn't enough, but it does give your child important models to hear, see, try out, and learn from. In addition, you can serve as language backup. When he says or writes something, don't say it's wrong, but repeat it in a more acceptable way. Then, let it pass. It will serve as a model without being a turn-off.

Then, remember the editing stage. Writers and public speakers edit—and do this last. Just like the rest of us, when your child speaks or writes it's almost always a "first draft" that came out when he was focusing on the ideas, not the spelling, grammar, or organization. It's hard to focus on all of these things at once. So see if you can wait until your child has gotten the ideas out and is ready to fine-tune how it sounds—in writing or speech. If it's a homework assignment or school paper, set up an editing time. Have a dictionary online or in book form and also a thesaurus and any other useful reference material handy. Ask your child to begin to edit the work by marking parts where there is spelling (or language or organization) he's not sure of. We all have questions and second thoughts about some of the language constructions we use, and help at this stage can feel good, so make it feel natural. Then you can do the next step together, in part using the reference material and in part making suggestions—it depends on your child, the moment, and what's right for him. Editing is a way to help your child focus on the smaller parts of language, to develop an ear for what might not sound "right," and to become familiar with resources to use for help, including yourself and others. But don't treat everything this way—it's too cumbersome. Only the papers and speeches that will go public, where the fine-tuned language use will count a lot and your child will feel good for having done it, need this level of re-doing.

Lastly, find out what the teacher is doing and how you can help.

CONNECTING WITH SCHOOL

Question #5: How can I help my child's teacher see what she's really like and really knows? For example, the teacher says she is very quiet in class, doesn't discuss, and needs to be drawn out—also that she doesn't read much. But at home she's extremely friendly and talkative, reads far above grade level, and discusses lots of ideas. It's as if we're talking about two different children.

Answer: It's not as if one of you is right and the other wrong. Children don't necessarily behave the same way at school and at home, and the reading and writing activities and social interactions aren't the same either. Both you and the teacher need to hear the other part of the picture so you can work together to help your child participate and do well in both settings.

Set up an appointment to meet with the teacher. State your concern, without being defensive. Then take turns describing the reading, writing, and social behaviors each of you has seen; give specific examples. Before discussing, each of you must listen to the other. Believe each other, but also be prepared to fill in the other part of the story. If possible, bring work (such as books your child has read and writing she's done) from home, and ask the teacher to show you the books she's read and writing she's done at school. See if, together, you can each understand the fuller picture and mutually develop a plan of action that might help her become a more active learner at school. Sometimes simply setting up a more constant home–school connection (such as I discussed above) helps. Sometimes the teacher can pair your child with a partner to read, write, and discuss with, and then build into a larger group. Knowing of your child's success at home, the teacher might put her in charge of a research team that can work and report together on a project. The goal will be for the teacher to take advantage of your child's knowledge while being sensitive to her reticence—to get her hooked into activities that require her to use what she knows, learn more, and feel comfortable and successful.

Question #6: How do I talk with the people at school in order to really help my child? I want to get them to respond, without causing problems for him.

Answer: Sometimes parental concerns have to do with some aspect of their child's life in a particular classroom, and at other times the problem involves a whole teaching team or school. You need to decide which it is before taking action. Let's start with the first. Parents get frustrated when their child is having social, learning, or other problems at school or when they're uncomfortable about something that's happening in class and feel nothing is being done about it. Sometimes they hold back too long, for fear of making it hard on their child, and anger or resentment builds. And then unhappiness comes out in negative rather than constructive ways. Instead, set up a meeting with the person involved at school. You'll need to figure out with whom, based on the problem. Choose the person you think is most responsible for the situation that is bothering you and thus most able to help. If you're not sure or are uncomfortable raising the issue, see the person you're most comfortable with and enlist his or her aid. Eventually, if not at first, all the people who can be helpful in planning a course of action need to meet, agree on what to do, monitor what is happening, and keep in touch—as I describe in Chapters 6 and 7.

But some problems are broader, involving a committee (e.g., scheduling, requirements, curriculum, or testing) or the entire school (e.g., school safety, discipline, bus schedules, extracurricular activities, or equipment), and are best taken up with and by school committees or the PTA. If you're not on any of these committees, you need to find out who is and how you can get to speak. Many committees have open meetings where people can raise questions. This is a good place to start. The school secretary should be able to tell you who is on the committee with responsibility for your concern and also whether it accepts visitors. If not, you can call or write to the chair, voicing your concern, asking if committee is working on the problem, and volunteering to help. If this doesn't work, you can always contact the administrators in charge, discuss it with them, and see if you can get more people involved. If these don't work, you can attend an open school board meeting or write a letter to the president of the board. In each instance, it's better to come prepared with more than a gripe—bring a description of your concern and a suggested plan for action. It will be a place to start, likely modified by the people you enlist to work with you. You need to work together. In many cases a committee will need to take on the problem or a new committee formed to investigate the matter, look into possible solutions, and make recommendations. While these matters take time, they lead to long-term change. Of course, if the problem requires immediate action, go right to the principal.

If your interactions with the school are positive, helpful, and collegial, you have no reason to be concerned about causing problems for your child. If your interactions are argumentative and accusatory, you will help no one, you'll exacerbate your unhappiness and convey it to your child, and you won't solve the problem.

Question #7: What can parents do to help their child have the best school experiences and what can they do to compensate for areas where the school falls short?

Answer: There are two ways you can approach this problem. The first is school based, the second is home based, and there's something you can do about both. Let's look at the school-based issue first. What you can do to shore up the school in ways you and other parents would like. Too often we think we need to accept things as they are, and that isn't so. Schools usually welcome ideas for enrichment, particularly when community members are willing to help. Decide whether your concern has to do with school facilities, programs and materials, extracurricular activities, and so on. Get on committees if they exist, and get them started if they don't (see

Chapter 8 for some ideas). You can learn what's possible, apply for grants, experiment with new ideas, get new things going. When parents and the community work along with schools, tremendous things are possible.

On the other hand, there are particular families that want particular kinds of experiences for their children that the larger group might not share. Setting up smaller home-based communities of interest is a more appropriate action. For example, a colleague of mine and her husband are Estonians and wanted their children to grow up bilingual. There were almost no other Estonian children at their school, but there was a small Estonian community of which they were a part. At her instigation, a group of parents began a language club for their children, when they would spend time together and speak only in Estonian. The same can be done with special interests in art, chess, literature, or whatever enrichment you're looking for. Ask the school or PTA about other parents who might be interested.

Question #8: What can you do to help your child in a school that doesn't have particularly high expectations and isn't particularly interested in raising them?

Answer: Unfortunately, some schools still sell children short and don't offer a program that's as challenging or enriching as some parents would like. If you have chosen your child's school, is this the best one for you and your child? If you have no choice or can't change, I'll assume you've already gotten to know and work with like-minded parents and teachers to try to get them to raise expectations. Committee members can visit other schools, review curriculum, see instruction in action, and get ideas about the kinds of curriculum and instruction higher expectations call for. Clearly, teachers and administrators will need to be involved, since they'll have to act on the ideas and convince others of their value. This is a way to begin to make changes in the essential program, in your child's day-to-day school experiences, and the most effective way to try to make change.

You can also look into setting up after-school clubs and activities that offer enrichment and challenge. They can focus on the academic subjects at school but, for extra fun and challenge, could also involve community members who can offer special knowledge (e.g., foreign-language instruction) and local agencies that can offer on-site, hands-on activities (in the offices of the local architect, newspaper, etc.). If money is available (or a grant arranged), local people could be hired to teach the courses. But they can work with volunteers as well. A parent and school committee can oversee the offerings and quality, and recommend change. Sometimes, when they see how much students can accomplish in such activities, even reluctant schools raise their expectations.

As I've described in this book, a combination of enriched school-based and community-involved activities works best.

WHY THINGS GET TAUGHT THAT WAY

Question #9: School is different today from when I was a student. What does it mean to say it's not enough to know the answers but that you need to do something with the information? What does it mean to have more than one right answer?

This question is related to another one I'm frequently asked:

Question #10: What is the current prevailing educational philosophy that's driving schools (or the range of philosophies), how do they play out in the classroom, how do they differ from what we ourselves experienced, and how can parents figure out which approach works best for our individual children?

I'll answer both at once.

Answer: A major body of research in the second half of the 20th century made educators aware that for new knowledge to be useful, it needs not only to be connected to what students already know but also needs to be thought about and dealt with in a variety of situations; mental links need to be made and networks built. It's related to the generative thinking that I discussed in Chapter 5 and is one of the instructional strategies teachers in more successful schools use to support learning. Over the long haul, memorization and recitation (the kind of instruction many of us had) doesn't cut it as well. Students can study and remember particular information for a test the way we did, but if the knowledge has nowhere to go in the brain, it's relegated to short-term rather than long-term memory. On the other hand, when knowledge is put to use, it becomes linked to the purposes for which it is being used (or can be used) as well as with effective strategies for using it; it's brought into a more stable network of useful and related ideas and knowledge.

Another major body of research led educators to see that the reader and the context, as well as the material (or text) being learned, contribute to what people understand. Who you are, the purpose for which you're reading or writing, as well as the piece itself and the social conditions in which it was written and is being read all make a difference in the understandings a person will come away with. For example, most of us read and understand Charles Dickens, Zora Neal Hurston, Gabriel Garcia Marquez, Lao Tse, or Virginia Wolf differently from our parents and even differently from when we read them 10 or 20 years ago. You may also come away from *A Christmas Carol, Mine Eyes Are Watching God, One Hundred Years of Solitude, Tao Te Ching,* or *Giovanni's Room* with different interpretations based on where you grew up, your religious and social experiences, and other reading you may have done. That's why books and plays are read and produced time and again, always with a slightly different interpretation. To take different perspectives is a way to help students develop into deeper readers who can gain layers of possible meaning from a text. It's what makes texts memorable and what makes readers and writers more thoughtful or thought provoking.

These views have helped generate major changes in education, the kind these questions deal with. Although there are philosophical camps (I discuss them in Chapters 5 and 8 and elsewhere in this book), almost everybody agrees that all students can and need to be helped to become more thoughtful learners who know a lot, who can deal with ideas deeply, and who can use what they know in a range of situations—many of which won't come up until later in their lives. Schools that work well value this kind of thinking and help all students learn to do it.

Question #11: Why does conversation matter so much in the classroom? My child is quiet and doesn't like to talk.

Answer: There is also a large body of related research that has influenced how educators treat conversation in the classroom. It deals with the relationship between language and thought, and has let us understand that genuine conversation in the classroom is a boost to learning; it helps students develop and refine their understandings. It becomes a time when students have a chance to try out and develop ideas. In order to talk, they need to think things through, make some sense of what the ideas mean and how they relate to other ideas. They need to find the words as well as the kinds of organization appropriate for talking about those ideas. Conversation requires extra thought about what's being learned. Also, during conversation, students have a chance to hear, to explain what they know, and to discover what they cannot explain (and probably don't yet understand). They can agree and disagree with one another, getting ideas they hadn't thought of themselves. These, too, help students get more deeply into the material. Discussion is one way to put new ideas to use and help them grow.

What about the quiet child? During class conversations, not all students speak all the time. They don't even speak all the time in small groups—no more than you always speak in a group after you have all seen a movie and are discussing it. Your mind keeps going, even if you say nothing. What counts in class discussion is that students are "minds-on," thinking about what's being said and using it to refine their ideas. Classes that stress conversation are interested in what everyone has to say about the topics discussed because classtime is used to develop further understandings. It is a time to explore ideas rather than to see if each student has the "right" answer. When students realize this, they usually speak when they have something to say.

Question #12: I didn't send my child to school to use her imagination, speculate about meanings, or think about multiple perspectives. How will that get her into college or land a good job?

Answer: I think I answered part of this in Questions 10 and 11. But let me deal with the issue of imagination. Research tells us that imagination is a useful way to solve problems both at school and in life, and is an important part of the well-developed mind. It's different from logical thinking and can lead to useful solutions. It takes you beyond the scope of the problem being addressed and gets you to explore new possibilities. It leads to breakthroughs. For many years, Japanese educators have been interested in American education. They say that Japanese education teaches the knowledge needed to produce highly complex products but that American education trains its students to be more creative, more imaginative— to imagine new products and uses and to take us where we haven't been. Both kinds of thinking are important, and both need to be taught at school.

And so, yes, with a well-rounded education that has developed both kinds of thinking (most schools still focus more on logical than creative thinking), your child should have a better chance to get into a good college and to land a good job. And once on the job, chances are your child will do better as well—not merely doing what is asked but also contributing to growth and development.

Question #13: Why use technology? I don't want to send my child to school to play games. Why should they use computers at school? I have one at home and restrict its use to writing.

Answer: This question treats computers the way people in Plato's time thought about writing. It was a time when writing was becoming prevalent in ancient Greece. Plato and others felt that if things were written down, people would lose their memories; relying on script, they wouldn't need to think any more. Looking back, we can see that writing and print became important tools for helping masses of people become literate, know more, and improve their lives. Memory wasn't eradicated, and literacy expanded the ways people thought. So, too, with computers. There are many uses for computers and many important ways of thinking that computers foster. Depriving students of the opportunity to gain these skills would be an error, since computers are becoming, and will likely continue to become, as pervasive a tool for thinking as script and print.

Using computers requires the ability to plan, use symbols, and work through abstract problems. Merely turning the computer on, learning its commands, planning and filling space on the screen, and correcting and fixing problems when things go wrong involve the use of visual relationships, hierarchical order, graphic memory, anticipation, organization, and a host of other abilities that are helpful in many kinds of learning, including but not limited to literacy and mathematics. Learning an array of computer functions and using them to produce a variety of texts extend a child's thinking even more. Reading, writing, and corresponding via the computer, as well as using the Internet for gathering information, open children to even more complex uses of knowledge, language, space, logic, and creativity. Using the computer to write, and also to gain information to write about, is an extremely important activity for children. It offers a way to write with greater ease and speed than the pen. It also permits important opportunities for refining ideas, organizing material, and trying out possible changes during the editing process.

But just as use of pen and print doesn't mean that every product is worthy of use, parents need to monitor computer content. Some games and instructional activities are banal, just busy work, but others help in all kinds of learning and add variety. For example, many computer games are challenging, leading a child to develop skills she doesn't practice much, like eye–hand coordination, strategizing, composing, embedding, and analyzing. But you don't want children playing computer games all the time, nor do you want them practicing the same skill all the time. Just as with other games your children play, plan for those that will be fun but also develop some skill and knowledge.

At school, computers are often used for research on the Internet as well as for notes taken from books in the library, for composing papers, and for keeping records. These are important activities that bring more content to your child but also require more complex filtering of what's relevant and where—important thinking, reporting, and writing skills. Also at school, some computer games are no better than skill-and-drill worksheets. They make minimal use of the technology and demand little in the way of complex thinking. But many software packages offer exciting opportunities for children to become engaged in high-level thinking involving concepts and skills they're learning in class.

Don't shortchange what computers can do for your child at home or at school. They offer new contexts and new uses for learning and give your child a leg up on the future. Because computers, however they may evolve, will be an integral part of children's adult lives, we need to see to it they become fluent in their uses and the ways of thinking they call upon.

SPECIAL NEEDS

Question #14: My child has a lot of trouble reading and writing. What can I do to help?

Answer: My first answer is one you've probably heard many times; it's as old as the hills and as true. A child who reads comes from a home that reads. Read to your child, but also read for yourself. Discuss books and articles you've read with your child and the people around you. Read together and discuss things both of you have read. See movies together and discuss them. Read stories, poems, or articles aloud, and talk about them. Enjoy literature with children of all ages and with everyone who lives at home. Try to keep up with your child. Read what he's reading at school and talk about what the pieces meant to you. Don't try to teach. Share. Enjoy. (That's teaching your child how to like and use books and make them part of his life.) When each Harry Potter book was released, I rushed out to get it. I knew my granddaughters who live in another state would be reading them, too, and I wanted to be able to discuss our mutual reactions during our regular phone calls. Older children can read to younger ones. When she was six, one of my granddaughters read many books to her little sister, months before she was born. And she continues to do it now. Study after study over time has shown that it's the literate home environment that makes a great difference in who reads well and who doesn't.

But even in the most reader-friendly environments, some children still have problems and need extra help. The earlier problems are detected, the better—but it's never too late. The moment you suspect your child is having difficulty, make an appointment to see the teacher. Sometimes it's attitude, sometimes work habits, sometimes needed background knowledge and skills, sometimes physical problems. Some problems are minor ones that you and the teacher can work on together. Some require specialists. Almost every school has a variety of specialists with particular training in a range of problems, including reading, learning, emotional, speech, and communication disorders. If the teacher suspects a problem, he will generally contact you and the relevant specialist. But if you suspect a problem, don't wait. Set up an appointment to see the teacher. Come with examples of the particular problems you've seen your child grapple with. The more detail you can supply, the better. The teacher can tell you what he sees in class. Together, decide upon next steps, perhaps including seeing the specialist, who may want to meet with your child and also observe him in class. Then, be sure there's a follow-up meeting as well as discussion of next steps. The specialist may suggest things for you and the teacher to do, may suggest special help at school, or may make an outside referral for further testing. If your child does receive special help at school, keep in touch with both the teacher and specialist. Get reports and try to help at home. School specialists are there to help you and to work with your child.

But this doesn't always work. If you want to go beyond the school for diagnosis or help, local universities almost always have reading, special education, and child development clinics with well-trained staffs ready to help. Other problems may be medical in nature and require a full physical or neurological checkup. If a medical problem is detected, there are many treatments and medications that can be extraordinarily helpful and change your child's academic learning dramatically. Whatever the problem, you need to find out and take action. The sooner, the better. If you need to go beyond the school for help of any sort and the school is not suggesting referrals, contact a nearby school of education, department of psychology, or medical school (whichever is most appropriate) and tell the secretary the kind of clinic or workup you're looking for. The secretary will generally refer you to someone who can help. Private specialists can also be helpful; it's best to get a referral. Follow through.

But even as these problems are being worked on by you and others, be sure to continue to keep the literate environment at home as rich as possible. Even if you don't see the payoff right away, the literacy learned through these informal encounters will echo through your child's life.

Question #15: What about students who are learning English as a second or third language? How different should their instruction be?

Answer: The most straightforward answer I can give is that at an essential level, there should be no difference at all. Every child needs to have high expectations, challenging material, an information-rich environment, and many opportunities to use language and discuss ideas in ever more complex ways. Most classes I've described in this book have some (and sometimes many) students for whom English is not their mother tongue. All of these students speak another language at home. In some schools, like

International High School (see Chapter 5), they are very recent immigrants. In most schools they have been in the United States for several years (we studied mainstream, not bilingual, classes). But the one thing they have in common is the quality of the professional environment and the quality of teaching they experience. Teachers know their students can understand the content (with help if needed) and share ideas even as they learn the language. They contribute to class and use it as a laboratory for language experimentation and use. They learn language and content at the same time.

Question #16: My child is bright but bored. What can I do and what can the teacher do to help?

Answer: My answer to this question will probably echo some of the things I've already said. I'll try to add, not repeat. First, be sure your child is really bored, not socially uncomfortable (feeling different from others or rejected), frustrated as a learner (and therefore opting out), or physically hampered (e.g., hearing or vision problems). These scenarios will take you on different paths, but all require attention. Talk to the teacher and develop a plan of action.

For me, a bored child is one who doesn't have any of these problems but already knows almost everything she is being asked to do in class and finds little to keep her interested and challenge her mind. It can also be a child who gets tired of doing the work in the same kind of way each time and needs variety. Boredom can be a real problem that turns potentially successful and even excellent students away from school. It isn't an inviting place for them to be. Children who get bored generally have already had a wealth of experiences at home, before school. These come from the child's own rich imaginative play or the experiences the family has provided (like the literacy-rich environments I discussed in Question 14).

If boredom is the problem, you must discuss it with your child's teacher. The teacher may see your child differently from you, and you need to discuss it. If your child is in fact bored, then together you need to find out whether the boredom is coming from the content your child is learning (does she already know it before it's being taught?) or from the format (e.g., being asked to write responses to everything she reads). If you and the teacher agree, invite your child to a conference. Ask her to help you figure out why she's bored and what would turn her on. Then the two or three of you can work together. For example, although your child does the same reading as everyone else, she (and perhaps another student or two) can be given a different assignment, one that expects them to do more generative thinking (Chapter 5) with and about the material. Or perhaps they can be assigned activities that get them moving as they think (e.g., research papers needing the Internet or library). Keep in touch with the teacher and your child. Discuss how things are going and which activities are working. Be sure to ask about enrichment activities that are offered during or after school. These are often connected to what your child is learning in class, but with higher expectations and greater enrichment. Remember also that most schools (or school districts) have special programs for the truly gifted. In some schools specialists work with groups of students at school, within the regular program, one or several times a week. Other schools have separate special programs for gifted students. Find out about them and, with the teacher, discuss whether these placements might be appropriate for your child. Also use this time to get to understand the class and the school from your child's perspective. Learn the school's philosophy and the teacher's approach. If things do not change, see whether you have options about class assignments and schools that are more appropriate for your child, places that would better meet your expectations about the kind of education she should receive.

IN CLOSING

The demands of education have changed and the stakes are higher—for teachers, administrators, and parents as well as for students. We can make curricular and programmatic modifications and add new offerings, but these won't bring about the essential re-visioning needed to make a long-lived difference in student learning. But if we dare to be bold, teachers, administrators, parents, and community members can work together as partners in re-creating our schools into active, energized, substantive, and informed workplaces and learning places where every student and educator has the opportunity to flourish. We can create better schools, and together get to excellent.

About the Study

I BEGAN THE STUDY on which this book is based when the standards and testing movement was beginning to take hold across the country and teachers and administrators were trying to respond to calls for the improvement of student performance—some more successfully than others. In an attempt to help, I wanted to learn what makes some schools particularly successful and other, comparable ones less so. I wanted to specify the professional environments that feed the knowledge educators draw on, the kinds of instruction students are experiencing, and how the larger community fits into the educational picture. Therefore the research focused on four "communities": the professional, programmatic, classroom, and neighborhood.

To maximize data gathering, the study took place over a 5-year period, permitting extended observations and interviews over time. The 5-year period also allowed us to collect data from schools in successive cohorts in several states. Each teacher, school, and situation was studied for 2 years, permitting extensive examination of how patterns within the professional, instructional, and local communities played themselves out and affected students over time. While the study focused on students and teachers in their English and language arts programs, the larger administrative and organizational structures and school and community experiences in which the teachers participated provided a broader backdrop to help us understand the related features that contribute to making schools work. Although our prime focus was on English, including reading and writing, some schools we studied (like other across the country) had been organized into cross-disciplinary academies, teams, and teaching collaborations (see, e.g., Chapter 4). These permitted our findings to have somewhat broader implications. However, findings from a study such as this can only serve as ideas and guidelines for others to use from the vantage points of their own particular localities, subject areas, and realities.

CRITERIA FOR SELECTION

The study took place in California, Florida, New York, and Texas, four states with very diverse student populations, educational problems, and approaches to improvement, as well as different testing demands. To identify potential sites, my research team and I asked educators from state education departments and professional organizations, as well as teachers and administrators, to recommend schools and teachers from the range of schools—urban, rural, and suburban—that were trying hard to be responsive to public concerns. Those identified for further consideration were nominated by at least three independent sources as places where professionals were working to improve student performance and test scores in reading, writing, and English. We then checked each state education department's website to identify those schools that were scoring higher than schools with similar student bodies as well as those that were scoring more typically, more like demographically similar schools. In each case, we examined literacy-related test data that carry high stakes for the teachers and administrators as well as the students and their parents. Schools whose performance on the high-stakes tests was markedly above that for schools serving demographically similar populations were designated for this book as those that were "working well." Referencing of scores against those from schools serving similar student populations allowed us to control for the overall tendency for higher-performing schools to be wealthy and suburban.[1]

We wished to identify the features contributing to making schools work across a range of demographic areas (urban, suburban, and urban fringe), and schools in each of these categories were selected for further consideration. Because we were particularly interested in identifying features of excellence in schools and districts serving poor and culturally diverse students, these were more heavily sampled. We visited the most promising schools based on a combination of recommendations and test scores, and from those we made a final selection based on the teachers' and administrators' willingness to work with us over a 2-year period as well as the school's ability to contribute to the overall diversity in student population, problems, and locations in our sample.

In the end, 25 schools, 44 teachers, 88 classes, and some 2,000 students were selected to participate in the study, with a focus on one class for each of the teachers in each of two consecutive years. Fourteen of the 25 participating schools were places that were "working well," performing better on state-administered high-stakes reading, writing, and English tests than schools rated as demographically comparable by statewide criteria. The other 11 schools were also places that had come highly recommended but had literacy scores more typical of other schools with similar demographics. Across the 25 schools, poverty levels ranged from 5 percent to 86 percent of the students receiving free or reduced-price lunches; student representation ranged from 92 percent African American and no White students in one school to 86 percent Hispanic and 2 percent White students in another, and the range between. The diversity is important, with some high-poverty and high-minority schools doing quite well.

DESIGN

The study involved a nested multicase design with each program as a case and the class including teachers and students as cases within. This design permitted shifting lenses among four contexts (professional, programmatic, classroom, and community), as ideas for instructional improvement were considered, discussed, and enacted.

PROCEDURES

Nine field researchers worked on the project with me; each gathered data in one or more schools for 2 years. This enabled us to study education in effective and more typical schools over 2 years, with two groups of students. The researches spent approximately 5 weeks per year at each school, including a week at the beginning of the year to interview district personnel, teachers, and students about their goals, plans, and perceptions. This was followed by 2 weeks each semester observing classes, conducting interviews, and shadowing the teachers in their professional encounters. We set up e-mail accounts or spoke by phone or in person in order to keep in weekly touch with teachers and students and to discuss classroom, professional, and parent–community school experiences. Student work was mailed to us weekly for use in the discussions.

DATA

Parallel sets of qualitative data were gathered at each of the sites. Data consisted of field notes of all observed meetings, classes, working groups, and conversations; e-mail messages; artifacts from school and professional experiences; tape recordings and transcripts of all interviews and observed class sessions; and in-process oral and written case reports developed by the field researchers. Three types of collaboration contributed to the development of the database: full project team, collaborative dyads, and case-study sessions. In addition to meetings with the participating teachers in each state, the full project's teachers and research team engaged in ongoing e-mail discussions about the activities, approaches, and progress in the participating classes and the teachers' professional experiences and their efforts to help their students do well. In addition, each teacher and field researcher communicated via e-mail approximately once a week to develop and reflect on the teacher's professional interactions as well as class sessions and student performance. Beyond this, the field researchers and I met weekly for case-study sessions. During these meetings, the field researchers presented in-process case-study reports about the professional networks, instructional activities and offerings, and parent and community involvement at their sites. These sessions offered opportunities for case-related patterns to be discussed, tested, and refined and for cross-case patterns to be noted for further recursive testing and analysis.

CODING

Coding was used to organize and index the various types of data in ways that permitted us to locate the participants' focus on key areas of concern. For example, where possible, all data were initially coded for the type of community the participants were focusing on or referring to—professional, classroom, neighborhood—as well as for their focus on instruction, curriculum, and assessment. More targeted codes for particular types of knowledge, skills, and processes were also used. This coding scheme served as an indexing system that allowed us to later retrieve and more carefully analyze data form one categorical subsection of the data pool, compare it with another, and generate data-driven subcategories for later analysis.

ANALYSES

Data were analyzed by a system of constant comparison, where patterns were identified and tested both within and across cases. We returned to each coded instance as well as to the full data set to qualitatively analyze the conditions under which each existed; this in turn led us to identify the features that differentiated the schools that work well from the others. The various data sets were keyed to the individual teacher, classroom, and school, providing multiple views of each instructional and educational context, permitting both in-depth case studies and cross-case perspectives to be developed. In each case, data were triangulated, drawing on various aspects of the three communities (professional, classroom, neighborhood) for evidence.

From our analyses, we came to understand the extent to which teachers and administrators were affected by the larger environment, leading to professional growth or malaise; the ways in which a wider and committed community of helpmates were involved or not; and the ways in which some schools were achieving unusually good educational results and others not.

From all this, I was able to identify particular features that were present in schools that work well but not in the others. The details of how things work in the more successful schools, including rich examples that can serve as models for change, form the substance of this book and can serve as inspection and anchor points for educators, parents, and community members who want to try their hand at *Getting to Excellent*.

Notes

CHAPTER 1

1. An ESEA primer, *Education Week*, January 9, 2002, www.edweek.com

2. State education departments have websites where information about their tests as well as student performance can be found.

3. Zernike, K. In high-scoring Scarsdale, a revolt against state tests, April 13, 2000, www.edweek.com; Manzo, K. K. Protests over state testing widespread, May 16, 2001, www.edweek.com; Tantraphol, R. Parents, teachers decry pressure, *Union News Sunday Republican*, March 7, 2000; Danitz, T. Mass. students revolt against mandatory graduation tests, retrieved February 14, 2002, from stateline.org (Stateline.org, an independent online publication of the Pew Center on the States, reports on issues involving state governments).

4. Smothers, R. (2002, February 8). New Jersey schools commissioner suggests eliminating some tests, *New York Times*, pp. B1.

5. For those who wish to read them, results of my studies were reported in the *American Educational Research Journal*, Winter 2001 (Excellence in English in middle and high school: How teachers' professional lives support student achievement) and Summer 2000 (Beating the odds: Teaching middle and high school students to read and write well). They were also published by the National Council of Teachers of English in a research monograph in 2002, *Effective literacy instruction: Building successful reading and writing programs*. Other articles and related materials based on the studies are online at cela.albany.edu. My additional studies and analyses from a broader perspective are the basis of this book.

6. In addition to my studies, see, for example, the Education Trust's "Dispelling the Myth" reports and online database at www.edtrust.org. This work targets low-performing and low-income schools.

7. See the appendix for a description of the selection criteria, design, and procedures used in the study.

CHAPTER 2

1. See, for example, Hortocollis, A. (2002, March 6). Boycotts and a bill protest mandatory state tests, *New York Times*, p. B9.

2. Some schools and districts in my study chose to have me use their real names and school names, while others requested anonymity. Throughout this book, I use actual names for those who granted permission and pseudonyms

for the others; I indicate which the first time a name is used. Parklane is a pseudonym.

3. Rachel Kahn is a pseudonym.

4. Miami/Dade County Public Schools is the actual name.

5. Hillocks, G. (2002). *The testing trap: How state writing assessments control learning.* New York: Teachers College Press.

6. Foshay Learning Center is the actual name.

7. Taylor, G., Shepard, L., Kinner, F., & Rosenthal, J. (2001). A survey of teachers' perspectives on high-stakes testing in Colorado: What gets taught and what gets lost. Retrieved January 23, 2002, from http://colorado.edu/epic/

8. The studies on which this book is based involved 88 classes in 25 schools that were compared based on demographic information provided on each state Education Department website.

CHAPTER 3

1. Darling-Hammond, L., & Ball, D. L. (1998). *Teaching for high standards: What policymakers need to know and be able to do.* Philadelphia: University of Pennsylvania: Consortium for Policy Research in Education and National Commission on Teaching and America's Future.

2. Parklane is a pseudonym, as are the names of people who work there.

3. Cathy Starr and Hudson are pseudonyms.

4. Green Path is a pseudonym.

5. The National Board Certification process requires candidates to submit evidence of a high level of professional activity, knowledge of content as well as current pedagogy, and videos of their classes in action. It involves a year-long self-examination and evidence of one's teaching practices as compared with Board standards, analyses of students' progress, and special follow-ups offered to meet students' needs. For more information, see www.nbpts.org

6. Evangeline Turner is a pseudonym.

7. The percent of students eligible for free or reduced-cost lunches is often used as an estimate of the economic status of the school community.

8. Suzanna Matton and Springfield High School are pseudonyms.

9. Both Sallie Snyder and Miami/Dade County Public Schools are actual names.

10. Alicia Alliston is a pseudonym.

CHAPTER 4

1. Cuban, L. (1984). *How teachers taught: Constancy and change in American classrooms.* New York: Teachers College Press. See also Tyack, D., & Cuban, L. (1997). *Tinkering toward utopia.* Cambridge, MA: Harvard University Press.

2. Both Connie McGee and the Miami/Dade County Public Schools are actual names.

3. Elmore, R. F. (2000). *Building a new structure for school leadership*. Washington, DC: Albert Shanker Institute.

4. See, for instance, McLaughlin, M., & Talbert, J. (1993). *Contexts that matter for teaching and learning*. Stanford, CA: Center for Research on the Context of Secondary School Teaching, Stanford University; and Talbert, J., & Perry, R. R. (1994). *How department communities mediate mathematics and science reforms*. Stanford, CA: Center for Research on the Context of Secondary School Teaching, Stanford University.

5. Newmann, F. (1991). Linking restructuring to authentic student achievement, *Phi Beta Kappan*, 72(6), 458–463. See also Elmore, R. (2002, January/February). The land of change, *The Harvard Education Letter*. Cambridge, MA: Harvard Graduate School of Education.

6. Parklane Middle School and Rachel Kahn are both pseudonyms.

7. Eija Rougle is the actual name; she is a researcher and instructional facilitator at the National Research Center on English Learning & Achievement.

8. In addition to International High School, discussed below, see Chapter 6 for mention of Hudson's schools within a school (called houses) and also Chapters 3, 5, and 6 for discussion of Springfield's academies and magnets.

9. There has been a great deal of research on school size. In a recent review, Kathleen Cotton found that most often students do better in small rather than large schools. Understanding the effectiveness of smaller communities of teachers and students who can get to know one another better and spend their time together in programs that are more responsive to students' learning needs, many large schools across the country have reorganized into houses or academies. Here, at least one teacher in each academic subject area and a designated number of students work together as an instructional body. Although they also have opportunities to interact with the larger school as a whole, their academic home is in their "school within a school." While smaller schools don't need to do this, larger schools that are higher-performing have established these smaller entities as a way of creating the opportunity for the kinds of collaborative environments I have been discussing. See Cotton, K. (2001). *New small learning communities: Findings from recent research*. Portland, OR: Northwest Regional Laboratories.

10. International High School is the actual name.

11. Marsha S. Slater is the actual name.

12. Snyder, S. (1999). *Beating the odds over time: One district's perspective* (CELA Report Series No. 12004). Albany, NY: National Research Center on English Learning & Achievement.

13. Richard Elmore calls this a culture of shared values that is not necessarily written down but "expressed in the words and actions of the people in the system." See Elmore, R. F. (1997). Investing in teacher learning. New York: Teachers College, Columbia University, National Commission on Teaching and America's Future, p. 8.

14. Tawanda Richardson, Alicia Alliston, and Charles Drew Middle School are pseudonyms.

15. Helen Clark is a pseudonym.

16. Hudson Middle School is a pseudonym.

CHAPTER 5

1. Cohen, D. K., & Ball, D. L. (2001). Making change: Instruction and its improvement, *Phi Delta Kappan, 83*(1), 73–77.

2. For details on how the envisionment-building classroom works, see Chapter 5 of Langer, J. (1995). *Envisioning literature: Literary understanding and literature instruction.* New York: Teachers College Press.

3. See Langer, J. (1990). The process of understanding: Reading for literary and informational purposes. *Research in the Teaching of English, 24*(3), 229–260.

4. Suzanna Matton and Springfield High School are both pseudonyms.

5. Celeste Rotundi is a pseudonym.

6. Both Kate McFadden-Midby and Foshay Learning Center are actual names.

7. They've actually done this all along. For historical review of research in writing and reading instruction, see Langer, J., & Allington, R. (1992). Curriculum research in reading and writing. In P. Jackson (Ed.), *Handbook of research on curriculum* (pp. 687–725). New York: Macmillan.

8. For a detailed explanation of separated, simulated, and integrated activities, see Langer J. (2000). Beating the odds: Teaching middle and high school students to read and write well, *American Educational Research Journal, 38*(4), 837–880.

9. For discussions of the successful kinds of help parents give to their children, see Halliday, M. A. K. (1977). *Learning how to mean.* New York: Elsevier; and Olson, D. (1985). See! Jumping! Some oral antecedents of literacy. In H. Goelman, A. Oberg, & F. Smith (Eds.), *Awakening to literacy* (pp. 185–192). London: Heinemann. For some of the kinds of help teachers can give, see Applebee, A. N., & Langer, J. A. (1983). Instructional scaffolding: Reading and writing as natural language activities, *Language Arts, 60*(2), 168–175.

CHAPTER 6

1. Delpit, L. (1995). *Other people's children: Cultural conflict in the classroom.* New York: New Press.

2. Springfield High School is a pseudonym.

3. Henry Hudson is a pseudonym.

4. The study focused on schools, not school districts. But in the case of high-performing small districts like the one Hudson was in, where there was only one middle and one high school, the district and schools worked both collaboratively and separately to involve parents in substantive ways.

5. New York State Education Commissioner's Regulation 100.11

6. Cathy Starr is a pseudonym.

CHAPTER 7

1. Both Ruby and Lincoln are pseudonyms, as are the teachers' names.

CHAPTER 8

1. Broder, D. S. (2002, April 28). A matter of money. *Washington Post*, p. B7.

2. Gene Carter, executive director of ASCD. Statement on teacher quality. Retrieved June 13, 2002, from www.ascd.org

3. Smith, C. (2002, June 14). Talks would tie schools & communities. *Charleston Daily Mail*, p. P7A.

4. See, for example, Aspiazu, G. G., Bauer, S. C., & Spillett, M. D. (1998). Improving academic performance of Hispanic youth, *Bilingual Education Research Journal*, 22(2), 1–20; Chavin, N. F. (1993). Families and schools in a pluralistic society. Albany: State University of New York Press; Floyd, L. (1998). Joining hands: A parental involvement program, *Urban Education*, 33(1), 123–35; and Lucas, T., Henze, R., & Donato, R. (1990). Promoting the success of Latino language-minority students: An exploratory study of six high schools, *Harvard Educational Review*, 60(3), 315–340.

5. See Grossman, P., Thompson, C., & Valencia, S. W. (2002). Focusing the concerns of new teachers: The district as teacher educator. In A. M. Hightower, M. S. Knapp, J. A. Marsh, & M. W. McLaughlin (Eds.), *School districts and instructional renewal: Opening the conversation* (pp. 129–142). New York: Teachers College Press.

6. I briefly present some suggestions for effective instruction in the following booklet: Langer, J. A., with Close, E., Angelis, J., & Preller, P. (2001). *Guidelines for teaching middle and high school students to read and write well*. Albany, NY: National Research Center on English Learning & Achievement, State University of New York at Albany.

7. Peterson, K. (2002). Changing school culture, *Journal of Staff Development*, 23, 3.

8. Killion, J. (2001). *Islands of hope in a sea of dreams: A research report of schools that received the National Award for Model Professional Development*. San Francisco: WestEd.

9. Moll, L. (1992). Funds of knowledge for teaching, *Theory into Practice*, 31(2), 132–41.

10. Hayward, E. (2002, June 19). Middle school dropout rate up, *Boston Herald*, p. 3. See also, Advocates for Children of New York and the New York Immigration Coalition. (June 2002). *Creating a Formula for Success: Why English Language Learners are Dropping Out of School and How to Increase Graduation Rates*. http://www.advocatesforchildren.org

APPENDIX

1. For example, for breakdowns of student performance, see National Assessment of Educational Progress (1994). *NAEP 1992 Writing Report Card*. Washington, DC: U. S. Government Printing Office.

Index

Academic programs
  and administrators, 31, 32, 35, 36, 72, 73, 84
  and aims/goals, 33, 35, 36, 72
  and collaboration/teamwork, 32, 33, 34, 36–37, 38–39
  and curriculum, 32, 33, 35, 36, 37, 38, 39, 72
  within department, 31–33, 34, 40, 72, 73
  and feedback, 36
  and frequently asked questions, 98
  and instruction/teaching, 34–37, 39, 40, 73
  within interdisciplinary team, 33–34
  and learning, 33, 34, 35, 39, 40
  and literacy, 31, 34, 72
  in magnet schools, 33
  and organization and structure, 34
  and parents, 38
  and philosophy/shared vision, 35–36, 37, 72
  and professional development, 39, 80
  and professionalism, 22
  and reform/change, 31–32, 77, 78, 80, 81, 84, 106
  and self-reflections of schools, 36
  and standards, 33, 36, 37, 72
  and teachers, 31, 32, 33, 35, 36, 37, 38, 39, 40, 72, 73, 81
  and testing, 31, 32, 36, 39, 40, 70, 73, 81
  tune-ups for, 30–41
  and two schools in one neighborhood, 70, 72–73
  See also Enrichment programs; Extra help
Academies, 37, 39, 59–60
Accountability, 2, 12
Administrators
  aims/goals of, 16, 83, 84
  caring by, 68
  and characteristics of effective schools, 6
  and choice of schools, 92
  common expectations about, 5
  dedication of, 35
  and frequently asked questions, 92, 97, 98
  functions of, 5
  involvement of, 16, 17, 24, 25, 26, 55, 68, 98
  and national focus on education, 2
  and parents, 84, 85
  and reform/change, 31, 78, 79, 81, 83–85, 86, 88, 106
  and school cultures, 83
  and two schools in one neighborhood, 66, 67–68, 69, 70, 71, 72, 73, 75, 76
  See also specific topic
Aims/goals
  and academic programs, 33, 35, 36, 72
  of administrators, 16, 83, 84
  and characteristics of effective schools, 6
  of community, 54, 78
  of curriculum, 11
  excellence as, 32
  of instruction, 21, 42–52
  for learning, 12–13
  and parents and community, 54, 68
  and professional development, 16
  and reform/change, 77, 78, 79, 83, 84, 87
  state and national, 6, 79
  and testing, 10, 11, 16, 81, 87
  and two schools in one neighborhood, 68, 72
  well-educated child as, 54
Alliston, Alicia, 27, 36
Annenberg Foundation, 84
Answers
  right answers to, 43, 47, 73, 79, 99, 101
  that teachers want, 43, 73
Apprenticeship, learning as, 46, 48
Assessment, 59, 89. See also Tests/testing
Association for Supervision and Curriculum Development, 80

"Best practices," 6
Boredom, of children, 105–6
Bossard, Norma, 11
Bush, George W., 2–3
Business Advisory Council, 86
Business community, 6, 60, 61, 68, 78, 85–86

California Literature Project, 25
California Writing Project, 25
Caring, 6, 63–64, 68, 78, 87
Change, educational. *See* Reform/change, educational
Charles Drew Middle School (California), 36
Children. *See* Students
Choice of schools, 90–93, 98, 106
Civic organizations, 60, 62
Clark, Helen, 36–37
Classrooms
   and choice of schools, 91–92
   conversation in, 100–101
   and frequently asked questions, 91–92, 96–97, 99–101
   and instruction/teaching, 74
   problems in, 96–97
   and reform/change, 4, 79, 81, 82
   testing in, 86–87
   and two schools in one neighborhood, 67, 74
Climate. *See* Environment
Collaboration/teamwork
   and academic programs, 32, 33, 34, 36–37, 38–39
   and administrators, 83, 84
   and characteristics of effective schools, 6
   and community and parents, 54–57, 58, 68, 85, 86
   and frequently asked questions, 93
   and problems of effective schools, 7
   and professionalism, 20, 21, 22, 23, 25, 26, 28, 71
   and reform/change, 79, 81, 82, 83, 84, 85, 86, 87
   among students, 82
   and testing, 17, 87
   and two schools in one neighborhood, 68, 71
Collins, Viola, 74, 75
Colorado, testing in, 16
Coming-to-understand process, 43
Committees, school, 97–98

Community
   and administrators, 55, 56, 57–58, 59, 61, 69, 78, 84–85
   aims/goals of, 54, 78
   caring, 63
   and characteristics of effective schools, 6
   and children's school lives, 57–59
   and collaboration, 85, 86
   culture of, 63
   and feedback, 78
   and frequently asked questions, 98
   of interest, 98
   involvement of, 2, 53–64, 68–69, 78, 80, 84–85
   and national focus on education, 2
   of professionals, 20, 21–24, 28, 71, 78, 83
   and reform/change, 4, 77, 78, 79, 80, 83–86, 88, 106
   reputation of, 54
   and school-based management, 54–57
   schools as central part of, 53–54
   schools as resource for, 54, 62–63
   and teachers, 55, 57, 58, 59, 61, 63, 69
   teachers as, 27–28, 77, 78, 79, 83–84
   and testing, 21–24
   and two schools in one neighborhood, 66, 68–69, 75
   See also Business community
Community service programs, 60
Computers, 101–3
Connecting with schools, 6, 94, 95–99
Content, 6, 20, 46, 47, 50, 51, 79, 82, 102, 105
Conversation, classroom, 100–101
Cramming, for tests, 5, 8, 14
Cuban, Larry, 31
Cultures, school, 83–84
Curriculum
   and academic programs, 32, 33, 35, 36, 37, 38, 39, 72
   and administrators, 16
   aims/goals of, 11
   building, 15–16
   common expectations about, 5
   and community and parent involvement, 59, 86
   feedback about, 15, 16
   and frequently asked questions, 89, 98
   and instruction/teaching, 48
   and national focus on education, 2–3
   as ongoing work-in progress, 16

and professional development, 17
and professionalism, 23, 24, 26
and reform/change, 6, 81, 82, 86, 106
and special needs, 38
and teachers, 15, 16, 17, 81, 82
and testing, 3, 8–18, 70, 81, 82
and two schools in one neighborhood,
    70, 72

Decision making, 6, 54–57, 84
Delpit, Lisa, 54
Departments
    academic programs within, 31–33, 34,
        40, 72, 73
    and community and parent
        involvement, 68
    and reform/change, 81
    and testing, 70
    and two schools in one neighborhood,
        68, 70, 72, 73
Diversity, 79–80
Donations to education, 78
Drilling, for tests, 14, 16, 82
Dropouts, school, 86

Education
    donations to, 78
    national focus on, 2–3
    as national priority, 78
    as set of interconnected processes, 4
Educational reform/change. *See* Reform/
    change, educational
Effective/excellent schools
    characteristics of, 1–2, 6, 78–81, 88
    problems of, 7
    and reform/change, 79–80, 81, 83, 85,
        86–87, 88
    See also specific school or topic
English and language arts
    and academic programs, 32, 35, 37, 38, 72
    and correcting child's grammar and
        spelling, 94–95
    and instruction/teaching, 74
    and reform/change, 81, 82
    and testing, 69, 70, 81, 82
    and two schools in one neighborhood,
        67, 69, 70, 72, 74–75
English as second or third language, 104–5
Enrichment programs, 37–40, 59–60, 72,
    91, 98, 106

Environment
    and administrators, 83, 84
    and choice of schools, 90, 91
    and frequently asked questions, 90, 91,
        104, 105
    home, 104
    and professionalism, 20, 21, 22–23, 26,
        28, 105
    and reform/change, 77, 78, 79, 80, 82,
        83, 84, 87
    and testing, 87
"Envisionment-building" instruction, 42–
    43, 44–45, 46, 47, 50, 51
Excellence, as aim/goal, 32
Expectations
    and administrators, 84
    and characteristics of effective schools, 6
    and choice of schools, 91
    common, 5
    and frequently asked questions, 91, 98,
        104, 106
    and reform/change, 79, 84, 87
    and special needs, 104, 106
    and testing, 87
Experience-based instruction, 48–51
Extra help, 37–40, 59–60, 72, 73, 91

Feedback
    and academic programs, 36
    and characteristics of effective schools, 6
    from community and parents, 57, 78
    and curriculum building, 15, 16
    and professionalism, 23
    and reform/change, 78
    from students, 15, 16
    from teachers, 15, 21, 36, 70
    and testing, 15, 16, 70
    and two schools in one neighborhood, 70
    and Writers in the Schools program, 39
Foshay Learning Center (Los Angeles,
    California), 15, 46–47
Frequently asked questions
    and choice of schools, 90–93
    and connecting with schools, 95–99
    and home decisions, 90–95
Funding. *See* Resources

Games, computer, 102–3
"Generative" learning, 44, 46, 51, 99, 105
Gifted/talented students, 39, 40, 105–6

Green Path (Texas school), 23
Grossman, Pam, 81

Henry Hudson Middle School (New York
    State)
  academic programs in, 38, 39
  as caring school, 63
  characteristics of, 55
  community and parent involvement at,
      55–56, 57–59, 60–61, 62, 63
  professionalism at, 23
  school-based management at, 55–56
Hillocks, George, 13
Home
  common expectations about, 5
  environment at, 104
  and frequently asked questions, 90–95,
      97–98
  schooling at, 68
Homework, 93, 95
Hudson Middle School. See Henry Hudson
    Middle School

Imagination, 101, 105
Individual educational plan (IEP), 38
Instruction/teaching
  and academic programs, 34, 35, 39, 40, 73
  and administrators, 16, 84
  aims/goals of, 21, 43–46
  building, 15, 16
  and coming-to-understand process, 43
  common expectations about, 5
  and community and parents, 46, 48, 49–
      50, 59, 68, 69
  and computers, 101–3
  and content, 46, 47, 50, 51
  and conversation, 100–101
  and correcting child's grammar and
      spelling, 94–95
  and curriculum, 48
  "envisionment-building," 42–43, 44–45,
      46, 47, 50, 51
  experience-based, 48–51
  and frequently asked questions, 89, 90,
      94–95, 98, 99–103, 104–5
  and imagination, 101
  improving, 51–52
  and integrated activities, 48–51
  and learning, 43, 44, 46, 47, 48–51, 74–
      75, 80

and literacy, 48, 49, 75
and national focus on education, 2–3
and organizing what gets taught, 34–37
and philosophy/shared vision, 48, 99–
    100
and professional development, 16–17,
    51, 80
and professionalism, 20, 21, 23, 24, 25,
    26, 71
and reform/change, 4, 6, 77, 78, 79–80,
    81, 82, 84, 87
as responsive to students, 42–52
and separated activities, 48–51
and simulated activities, 48–51
skills-based, 48–51
and standards, 48
and strategies for thinking, 46–48, 51, 99
and teachers, 16, 17, 43, 46, 48, 49, 51,
    73–75, 80, 81, 82
and teaching students what to do, 46–48
and testing, 11, 13, 14, 15, 16, 17, 44, 45,
    69, 70–71, 75, 82, 87
and thinking, 3, 46–48, 51, 82, 99, 101
and two schools in one neighborhood,
    66, 68, 69, 70–71, 73–75
variety of approaches in, 48, 51, 82
Integrated activities, 48–51
Interdisciplinary teams, academic
    programs within, 33–34
International High School (New York
    City), 33–34, 104–5

Justice, Vanessa, 74

Kahn, Rachel, 10–11, 22, 32, 33
Kennedy, Edward, 2
"Key lime pie" syndrome, 31
Killion, Joellen, 83–84

Lappin, Howard, 47
Learning
  and academic programs, 33, 34, 35, 39, 40
  and administrators, 27, 83–84
  aims/goals for, 12–13
  as apprenticeship, 46, 48
  and characteristics of effective schools, 6
  and choice of schools, 90, 92
  common expectations about, 5
  and community and parent
      involvement, 62, 85

and computers, 102
and frequently asked questions, 90–91,
   92, 93, 99–100, 102, 103, 105, 106
"generative," 44, 46, 51, 99, 105
in-depth, 82, 100
and instruction/teaching, 43, 44, 46, 47,
   48–51, 74–75, 80
life-long, 27
and national focus on education, 2, 3
and professional development, 80
and professionalism, 20, 21, 22, 25, 27–28
and reform/change, 4, 6, 31, 78, 79, 80,
   82, 83–84, 85, 86, 87, 88, 106
respect for, 27–28
and teachers as learners, 27–28, 77, 79,
   83–84
and testing, 3, 10, 70, 87
and thinking about students as learners,
   90–91
and two schools in one neighborhood,
   70, 74–75
Lincoln High School (Texas)
   academic programs at, 72–73
   instruction at, 73–75
   new teachers at, 71
   overview of, 65–68, 75–76
   parents and community at, 68–69
   professionalism at, 71–72
   testing at, 69–71
Literacy
   and academic programs, 31, 34, 72
   and computers, 102
   definition of, 9
   and frequently asked questions, 102, 104
   importance of, 4
   and instruction/teaching, 48, 49, 75
   and professionalism, 22
   and reform/change, 4, 81, 82
   statistics on, 9
   and teachers, 81, 82
   and testing, 8–9, 81, 82
   and two schools in one neighborhood,
      72, 75

McFadden-Midby, Kate, 15, 46–47
McGee, Connie, 31
Magnet programs/schools, 33, 59–60
Management and organization, school, 6,
   31, 34, 54–57, 68, 89, 90
Matton, Suzanna, 26, 44–45, 46

Mentors, 25, 59, 60, 71, 72
Miami/Dade County Public Schools
   academic program in, 35
   building curriculum at, 15
   characteristics of, 11
   and educational innovations, 31
   professionalism at, 27
   respect for learning at, 27
   and testing, 11–12, 15
Moll, Luis, 85
Multiculturalism, 80

National Assessment of Educational
   Progress, 2
National Board Certification, 24, 25
National Council of Teachers of English, 25
"Nation's Report Card," 2
Neighborhood, two schools in one, 65–76
No Child Left Behind Act (2001), 2–3

Open meetings, 97
Oregon, education in, 78
Organization and management, school, 6,
   31, 34, 54–57, 68, 89, 90

Parents
   and academic programs, 38
   and administrators, 55, 56, 57–58, 59, 61,
      69, 84–85
   aims/goals of, 54
   and characteristics of effective schools, 6
   and collaboration, 85, 86
   common expectations about, 5
   and compensating for limitations of
      schools, 97–98
   and curriculum, 86
   frequently asked questions by, 89–106
   and instruction/teaching, 46, 48, 49–50
   involvement of, 53–64, 68–69, 78, 80, 84–
      85, 91, 92, 96–98, 103–4
   keeping in touch with, 57–59, 83, 85, 93
   and learning, 85
   and national focus on education, 3
   problems and needs of, 61, 68, 83
   and professionalism, 22
   and reform/change, 77, 78, 79, 80, 83,
      84, 85–86, 88, 106
   and school lives of students, 57–59, 93,
      95–96
   school visits by, 91–93

Parents (*continued*)
  and school-based management, 54–57
  and special needs, 103–4
  and Strive for Success project, 38
  and students connecting with schools,
    95–96
  and teachers, 55, 57, 58, 59, 61, 63, 69, 85
  and testing, 3, 9, 11
  and two schools in one neighborhood,
    66, 67, 68–69
  See also Home
Parklane Middle School (Texas)
  academic program at, 32–33, 39
  building curriculum at, 15
  characteristics of, 10
  professionalism at, 22
  and testing, 10–11, 12, 14, 15
Peterson, Kent, 83
Pew Foundation, 84
Philosophy/shared vision
  and academic programs, 35–36, 37, 72
  and administrators, 84
  and choice of schools, 90
  and frequently asked questions, 90, 99–
    100, 106
  and instruction/teaching, 48, 99–100
  and professionalism, 21, 24, 28
  and reform/change, 84
  and special needs, 106
  and two schools in one neighborhood,
    72, 75
Piaget, Jean, 19
Principals. *See* Administrators
Privacy, of students, 93
Privatization of schools, 39, 68
Professional development
  and academic programs, 39, 80
  and administrators, 16, 17, 83–84
  and community and parent
    involvement, 69
  and curriculum, 17
  and instruction/teaching, 16–17, 51, 80
  and learning, 80
  and professionalism, 22, 24, 25
  and reform/change, 80, 82, 83–84
  resources for, 16–17
  and testing, 10, 16–17, 80
  and two schools in one neighborhood, 69
Professional networks, 21–22
Professional organizations, 24, 25

Professionalism
  and academic program, 22
  and administrators, 20, 21, 22, 23, 24, 25,
    26, 27, 71, 83–84
  and characteristics of effective schools, 6
  and collaboration/teamwork, 20, 21, 22,
    23, 25, 26, 28, 71
  and content, 20
  and curriculum, 23, 24, 26
  environment for, 20, 21, 22–23, 26, 28, 105
  and feedback, 23
  importance of, 3–7
  and instruction/teaching, 20, 21, 23, 24,
    26, 71
  and learning, 20, 21, 22, 25, 27–28
  and literacy, 22
  and parents, 22
  and philosophy/shared vision, 21, 24, 28
  and planning for future, 21
  and professional development, 22, 24, 25
  and professionals as community, 20, 21–
    24, 71
  and reflection, 23
  and reform/change, 4, 21, 24, 25–26, 79,
    83–84, 87
  and resources, 22, 28
  in schools that work, 28–29
  and sense of agency, 25–26
  and sense of community, 83
  and standards, 24, 26, 71
  and students' needs, 20–21, 25, 71
  and testing, 23, 24, 71, 87
  and two schools in one neighborhood,
    71–72
  within and beyond the school, 24–25
PTA, 55, 61, 97, 98

Questions
  and answers that teachers want, 43, 73
  frequently asked by parents, 89–106
  and learning, 82
  and reform/change, 82
  right answers to, 43, 47, 73, 79, 99, 101

Race, 2
Rating your school
  on academic programs, 40, 41
  on community and parent involvement,
    63, 64
  on instruction/teaching, 51, 52

on professionalism, 28, 29
on testing, 17, 18
Reading, 103–4
Reform/change, educational
   administrators' role in, 78, 79, 81, 83–85,
      86, 88, 106
   and aims/goals, 77, 78, 79, 83, 84, 87
   and "best practices," 6
   and caring, 78
   and diversity, 79–80
   failure of, 32
   and frequently asked questions, 100
   future of, 86–88
   importance of, 7
   and literacy, 4, 81, 82
   and national focus on education, 2–3
   parents' role in, 77, 78, 79, 80, 83, 84, 85–
      86, 88, 106
   and problems of effective schools, 7
   road to, 77–88
   and school cultures, 83–84
   teachers' role in, 4, 6, 77, 78, 79, 80, 81–
      84, 85, 86, 88, 106
   See also specific topic
Remediation, 38, 72. *See also* Extra help
Resources, 7, 16–17, 22, 28, 81, 84, 98
Respect, for learning, 27–28
Richardson, Tawanda, 36
Role models, 63
Rotundi, Celeste, 45, 46
Rougle, Eija, 32–33
Ruby Middle School (Texas)
   academic programs at, 72–73
   characteristics of, 66–68
   instruction at, 73–75
   new teachers at, 71–72
   overview of, 65–66, 75–76
   parents and community at, 68–69
   professionalism at, 71–72
   testing at, 69–71

School board, 97
Schools
   caring, 63–64
   children's lives in, 57–59, 93, 95–96
   choosing, 90–93, 98, 106
   as community resource, 54, 62–63
   connecting with, 6, 94, 95–99
   cultures of, 83–84
   discontent with, 2

general information about, 91
mandate for change given to, 4
marks of distinction among, 84
national focus on, 2–3, 203
offerings within and beyond, 59–62
organization and management of, 6, 31,
   34, 54–57, 68, 89, 90
self-evaluation/reflection of, 10–12, 36, 83
students' image of, 6
university partnerships with, 25, 37, 60, 84
visits to, 91–93
See also specific school or topic
Sense of agency, 25–26
Separated activities, 48–51
Shared vision. *See* Philosophy/shared
   vision
Simulated activities, 48–51
Skills-based instruction, 48–51
Slater, Marsha S., 34
Snyder, Sallie, 27, 35
Special needs, 38–39, 60–61, 103–6
Springfield High School (California)
   administrative style at, 26
   as caring school, 63
   community and parent involvement at,
      55, 57, 58, 59–60, 62, 63
   instruction in, 44–45
   overview of, 44
Standards
   and academic programs, 33, 36, 37, 72
   and administrators, 84
   and community and parent
      involvement, 54
   and instruction/teaching, 48
   and national focus on education, 2–3
   and professionalism, 24, 26, 71
   and reform/change, 2, 84, 87
   state and national, 2
   and testing, 11, 15, 16, 17, 69, 87
   and two schools in one neighborhood,
      69, 71, 72
Starr, Cathy, 22–23, 38, 39, 56
Stereotypes, 19–20
Strategies for thinking, 3, 46–48, 51, 82
Strive for Success project (Hudson Middle
   School), 38
Students
   at risk, 45
   behavior of, 67–68, 95–96
   boredom of, 105–6

Students (*continued*)
  connecting with schools, 6, 94, 95–99
  correcting grammar and spelling of, 94–95
  feedback from, 15, 16
  images of schools and teachers held by, 6, 19
  instruction as responsive to, 42–52
  involvement of, 69, 73
  needs of, 6, 20–21, 25, 71, 72, 79
  parents causing problems for, 96–97
  privacy of, 93
  quiet, 95–96, 100–101
  reports to parents about, 57–59, 83, 85, 93
  school lives of, 57–59, 93, 95–96
  and teaching them what to do, 46–48
  and two schools in one neighborhood, 66–68, 69, 71, 72, 73, 74
  See also specific topic
Success, student, 86–87
Summer schools, 37

Teachers
  and boredom of children, 105–6
  caring, 63
  and characteristics of effective schools, 6
  children's images of, 19
  and choice of schools, 92
  common expectations about, 5
  creativity of, 6
  dedication of, 35
  feedback from, 15, 21, 36, 70
  and frequently asked questions, 92, 93, 94, 95–96, 98, 105–6
  involvement of, 10, 16–17, 20, 21–22, 24, 25, 26, 36–37, 55, 68, 69–70, 81, 84, 98
  knowledge of, 20, 21, 25–26, 79
  as learners, 27–28, 77, 79, 83–84
  and national focus on education, 2, 3
  new, 69, 71, 72, 73, 84
  and problems of effective schools, 7
  and reform/change, 4, 6, 31, 77, 78, 79, 80, 81–84, 85, 86, 88, 106
  support for, 10–12, 26, 81, 84
  turnover of, 68, 69
  and two schools in one neighborhood, 66, 67, 68, 69–70, 71–72, 73–75
  See also specific topic

Teamwork. *See* Collaboration
Technology, 101–3
Tests/testing
  and academic programs, 31, 32, 36, 39, 40, 70, 73, 81
  and accountability, 12
  and administrators, 10, 13, 16, 17, 69, 70, 71, 83, 84
  and aims/goals, 10, 12–13, 81, 87
  as blueprint, 13
  class, 86–87
  and collaboration, 17, 87
  common expectations about, 5
  and community and parent involvement, 3, 9, 11, 69
  cramming for, 5, 8, 14
  and curriculum, 3, 8–18, 70, 81, 82
  and departments, 70
  differing focuses of, 8–9
  drilling for, 14, 16, 82
  and dropout rates, 86
  and environment, 87
  in excellent schools, 17–18
  and expectations, 87
  and feedback, 15, 16, 70
  functions of, 12, 13, 87
  high-stakes, 2–3, 8–18, 23, 44, 70–71, 81–82, 86–88
  increased emphasis on, 9
  and instruction/teaching, 11, 13, 14, 15, 16, 17, 44, 45, 69, 70–71, 75, 82, 87
  interpreting, 12
  and learning, 3, 10, 70, 87
  limitations/disadvantages of, 3, 9, 32
  and literacy, 8–9, 81, 82
  and multiple measures for assessment, 87
  and national focus on education, 2–3
  as opportunity, 10–12
  preparation for, 9, 11–12, 13, 14, 16, 17, 66, 70, 81–82
  and professional development, 10, 16–17, 80
  and professionalism, 23, 24, 71, 87
  and reform/change, 77, 80, 81–82, 83, 84, 86–88
  and resources, 16–17
  scores on, 5, 14, 15, 16, 31, 39, 40, 69, 70, 71, 75, 83
  and standards, 11, 15, 16, 17, 69, 87
  students' reactions to, 11, 14, 69

and teachers, 3, 10, 12–13, 15, 16–17, 69–70, 81–82
as time-sensitive, 9, 87–88
and two schools in one neighborhood, 66, 69–71, 73, 75
using results of, 11
Thinking
and frequently asked questions, 99–100, 101, 103, 105
and instruction/teaching, 3, 46–48, 51, 82, 99, 101
and reform/change, 79, 82
strategies for, 3, 46–48, 51, 82, 99
and two schools in one neighborhood, 73–74
Turner, Evangeline, 25

Tutorial help, 38, 39, 60, 72, 73
Tyack, David, 31

Universities
schools' partnerships with, 25, 37, 60, 84
and special needs, 104

Values, 67, 83
and reform/change, 83
See also Philosophy/shared vision
Volunteers, 98

Writers in the Schools program (Parklane), 39

Young, Shaney, 75

About the Author

JUDITH A. LANGER is Distinguished Professor at the University at Albany, State University of New York, where she is founder and director of the Albany Institute for Research in Education and director of the National Research Center on English Learning and Achievement. She is an internationally known scholar in literacy education. Her research focuses on the development of the literate mind—how people become highly literate, and ways in which education can help students become more effectively literate in school and life. Her major works examine the nature of literate thought— the knowledge students use to "make sense" and the ways in which their learning is affected by activities and interactions at school. She has studied reading and writing development, the ways in which understanding grows over time, disciplinary differences in reasoning and language use, how particular learning environments affect literacy learning, the effects of literacy instruction on academic learning, the contribution of literature to literacy, and the professional and classroom features that accompany effective learning. Her most recent research focuses on the kinds of professional and institutional procedures and activities that need to be put in place to improve student learning. Langer's work has had a strong impact on policy and practice. Related to this, she serves on many advisory boards and task forces seeking to improve student learning.

She is the author of numerous research reports, articles, chapters, and monographs; this is her tenth book. She sits on six editorial boards and has reviewed for 17 national and international journals. She has received many notable awards, among them appointment as Distinguished Professor, the highest rank in the State University of New York system; the State University of New York Chancellor's Award for Exemplary Contributions to Research; Distinguished Benton Fellow, University of Chicago; Fellow and Scholar-in-Residence, Rockefeller Foundation, Bellagio, Italy; Distinguished Visiting Scholar, University of Turku (Finland); and Presidential Award for Lifetime Achievement, Hofstra University. She has been inducted into the international Reading Hall of Fame.